Stories from Yantic Cemetery

Stories from Yantic Cemetery
by Melodye A. Whatley

Edited by Lynn Whiteford
Photographs by Melodye A. Whatley
Cover Design by Glenn Alan Cheney

Published by
New London Librarium
P.O. Box 284
Hanover, CT 06350
NLLibrarium.com

ISBNs:
13: 978-1517481285
10: 1517481287

Stories from Yantic Cemetery

Melodye A. Whatley

New London Librarium

Introduction

In doing the research for this book, I was surprised at the number of people who had died, or in some cases were buried elsewhere and were eventually brought back to Norwich, Connecticut to be buried in the Yantic Cemetery. We can give partial credit to Dr. Thomas Holmes, the 'father of modern embalming,' for without the embalming techniques developed during the Civil War era, it would have been impossible to transport bodies long distances and at the much slower pace than we now are familiar with.

It was Chester Hillard (found in the chapter on Mariners) that started me on my quest in the Yantic Cemetery. When I read "the only surviving passenger...," I knew there had to be a story there, and I just *had* to know that story. Then I questioned just how many more interesting people and fascinating stories must be waiting to be 'unearthed.'

Some people might ask, how did I pick and choose from such a huge cemetery? I know it would take several lifetimes to research all of those buried in Yantic. I have a number of the 'usual suspects': the Backuses, Osgoods, Slaters, etc. Some stories came from merely looking at the cemetery records (found on the Norwich City website), noting that the person had died elsewhere: Fort Benton, Montana (Edmund Bradley, Jr.); Chicago, Illinois (Timothy Blackstone); or George Ulmer who died in Crockett, California in 1907. I knew there *had to be a story there.*

Sometimes it was the unusual stone or statuary that drew me. Yantic Cemetery certainly does have many fine examples. Also the 'stones' that are not really stones (see the chapter on White Bronze).

I found the research portion of this project *fascinating*. I never knew just where the research would take me: from China (Edward Smith, missionary for 50 years) to the Chickasaw and Choctaw nations (Alvan Bond).

My poor husband has had to endure many hours of 'quiet disappearance' of his wife as I pored over documents, articles and websites while gathering interesting and often intriguing information.

I have used a number of resources. The Otis Library has been an invaluable resource, and I have spent many hours in the Genealogy Room poring over the microfiche as well as the *Norwich Stedman Directories*. The staff have been tremendously helpful. I was also blessed to be gifted with a copy of the *History of New London County, Connecticut* sans its front or back cover, but the pages of information as well as the wonderful lithographs have been of tremendous value.

The photographs in this book that are not documented as being from other sources were taken by myself during my research.

The Yantic Cemetery

The Yantic Cemetery is located on Lafayette Street in Norwich, Connecticut, just beyond the William W. Backus Hospital.

In the 1840's, with the filling of the Norwichtown Cemetery, the town saw the need for a new burial ground. The Yantic Cemetery was established on July 12, 1844 with pomp and circumstance. A dedication ceremony was held with Reverend Alvan Bond as the speaker, and the opening prayer was said by 'Mr.' Paddock (probably Reverend Benjamin Paddock) of the Episcopal church. Mr. Charles Thurber, a prominent hymn writer of the day, wrote two songs for the occasion and sang them that day. The first hymn began with "O thou who hast these spirits lit..." and the second hymn started out with "Take within thy keeping Father…"

The Yantic Cemetery was built on the style of a garden, popular during the Victorian era. There are circles and winding paths. It was meant as a peaceful place that the public could visit "in a spirit of solemn contemplation." [1]

Located near the entrance of the cemetery where the road forks to the left, is a map (pictured below). Although it may not seem so at first glance, the cemetery is laid out in a very organized fashion. The map, I do have to say, is probably about 85% accurate. Many times families would buy a family plot, but would

---

1 From the online article " *'An Interval With Tranquility': The Rural Cemetery Movement in the United States,"* from the website www.victoriangothic.org.

move away and the plot would be sold to another family. Therefore many sections/family plots are still as they are listed here, but some are not.

Just sixty years after the opening of the Yantic Cemetery, the town would once again find it necessary to acquire new grounds for the burial of its citizens. Maplewood Cemetery would be established in 1902, with the purchase of the former Osgood farm, but from 1844 (at least one stone dates much earlier) to the early 1900's, the Yantic Cemetery was *the* most common resting place for its citizens. Burials continued on a regular basis until the late 1900's, and even now family members may be buried in the Yantic Cemetery where there is a spot remaining in their family plot.

Table of Contents

I.

Authors, Writers and Publishers of the Written Word

Henry Bill (1824-1891)   Sect. 62-17

Henry Bill was born in Ledyard, Connecticut on May 18, 1824, the son of Gurdon and Lucy Bill.

Henry Bill began to work at the age of 15 for the *New London Gazette,* but soon returned to the Norwich area and began working as a teacher in the Broadbrook School in Preston, Connecticut. He attended the academy in Plainfield to complete his qualifications for teaching, and taught in the Plainfield and Groton schools for the next four years.

A family member, the Honorable James A. Bill, was involved in the publishing industry in Philadelphia and Henry decided to join him in that endeavor. For three years, Henry traveled through the western states for him.

In February of 1847, Henry Bill married Julia Octavo Chapman (1824-1903), of Groton, Connecticut.

Children:
- Henry Gustavus Bill (1847-1859)
- Lucy Bill (1849-1849)
- John Harper Bill (1851-1871)
- Henry Summer Bill (1856-1858)
- Julia Florence Bill (1858-); married Joseph H. Selden
- Jane Eliza Bill (also known as 'Jennie') (1860-1950)
- Frederic Abbott Bill (1864-1910)

3

The family moved back to Norwich and Henry Bill began his own publishing business, working closely with the Harper Brothers of New York. He was a publisher of what we now call 'coffee table' books. He continued to be involved with the Harper Brothers in New York until the year of his death in 1891.

Henry Bill is responsible for the building and development of the Laurel Hill section of Norwich, even donating property for a park in that area.[1]

The Chelsea Savings Bank in Norwich was incorporated in 1858. "The first deposit made [in the Chelsea Savings Bank] was that of Julia A. (Mrs. Henry) Bill, who entrusted $100 to the safekeeping of The Chelsea Savings Bank."[2] Henry Bill would later become president of this same bank and served in that capacity for two years (1888-1890).

Henry Bill died August 14, 1891. Julia outlived him a dozen years, and died November 19, 1903.

Painting of Henry Gustavus Bill (1847-1859) and John Harper Bill (1851-1871). Painted by Alexander Emmons. From the 1992 calendar designed and printed by Franklin Impressions, Inc.

1 *History of New London County, Connecticut, with biographical sketches of many of its pioneers and prominent men,* by Duane Hamilton Hurd, Philadelphia, J.W. Lewis & Co., p. 372.
2 *Historical Sketch of Banking, Norwich, Connecticut with Excerpts from Yesteryear,* by Severn T. Johanessen, 1976.

Allan Cleworth (1853-1906)

Allan Cleworth was one of the publishers of the *Norwich Evening Record*. In 1890, Cleworth and Frank Pullen purchased the paper (Frank Pullen is also included in this section). From the *Souvenir Edition, Norwich Evening Record,* published in 1894, we find this account of the beginnings of this publication: "Established May 22, 1888, as a political party organ, the *Norwich Evening Record* maintained a precarious existence for two years, during which it changed hands several times. On May 5, 1890, it became by purchase the property of its present owners, Messrs. Cleworth and Pullen… Their office and operation was located at 101 Broadway, downtown Norwich."

Allan Cleworth was born in September of 1853 in Massachusetts; both his parents, William and Nancy Cleworth, were from England. His wife Cora (Moulton) Cleworth was born in November of 1861 in Maine; her father, David Moulton, was from Maine and her mother, Alice, was from England.

Allan Cleworth and Cora E. Moulton were married December 21, 1881 in Manchester, New Hampshire. Their daughter Alice was born in May of 1884.

Allen Cleworth, *Norwich Evening Record: Souvenir Edition, reprinted 1993.*

Allan Cleworth died February 27, 1906. Cora Cleworth died in 1931.

Nettie Marie Bisbee Fanning (1863-1944)   Sect. 1-20

Nettie Marie (Bisbee) Fanning was born in Delhi, Delaware County, New York on March 12, 1863. Her husband John Earle Fanning was born in the Greenville section of Norwich on May 27, 1859. John was the son of George W. Fanning (1818-1887) and Martha M. Martin (1820-1887).

Nettie wrote a book titled *Uncle Gideon.* It was a thinly disguised biography of her husband's uncle, Uncle Gurdon Fanning, and reminisces of their visits with him and about life in the 'village.' He lived in Poquetanuck Village, Preston, just a few miles from Norwich.

She and John would ride their Rambler bicycles to Uncle Gideon's house. In her book she relates, "Outside the city one encountered stony hills and sandy levels, or dirt roads, rutty… and dusty or muddy depending on the weather. So when the newly-formed wheel club built a cinder bicycle path paralleling the river road there was general rejoicing."[3]

John and Nettie owned an artwork studio that was located at 31 Willow Street in Norwich (now a parking area) in the 1880's. According to the 1900 census, John was working as a rubber salesman.

John Fanning died May 18, 1929. Nettie Fanning died November 1, 1944.

---

3 *Uncle Gideon,* by Nettie Bisbee Fanning, Boston, Mass. : Stratford, ca. 1932.

Margaret Fuller (1872-1954)   Sect 15-15

Margaret Wittier Fuller, writer and playwright, was born in Brooklyn, New York on January 23, 1872, daughter of Captain James Ebenezer Fuller (1838-1912) and Rebecca Phyllis Hope Fuller (1844-1924). They moved to Norwich in 1874, when Margaret was about two years old. Her father James was, by then, an insurance agent in Norwich.

Fuller wrote *A New England Childhood* published in 1916 by Little & Brown of Boston; *Alma* the reprint edition published in 1927 by Grossett & Dunlap; and *The Complete History of the Deluge in Verse and Pictures* published in 1936 by Hawthorn House. She also wrote a play titled "Overnight", which was performed on stage in Norwich in 1935.

Margaret Fuller died on February 1, 1954 in Boston, Massachusetts.

Frank H. Pullen (1858-1927)   Sect. 76-15

Frank H. Pullen, co-owner of the *Norwich Record,* (Cleworth and Pullen publishing; see more about Cleworth in this section) was born in Massachusetts in October of 1858, the son of Weston and Mary Pullen of Lowell, Massachusetts.

His wife Annie L. (Carpenter) Pullen was born in Massachusetts in March of 1859, the daughter of Benedict and Francis Carpenter. They were married April 22, 1885. Their house was located at 52 Lincoln Avenue in Norwich, Connecticut.

In the 1900 census, five children are listed to them:

- Elizabeth F. Pullen, born February 1886
- Weston C. Pullen, born July 1888
- Benedict C. Pullen, born June 1890
- Marion L. Pullen, born September 1891
- Esther Pullen, born April 1899

Frank Pullen died December 2, 1927. Annie Pullen died January 2, 1932.

Frank H. Pullen, from the *Norwich Evening Record: Souvenir Edition, reprinted 1993.*

David Dwight Wells (1868-1900)　　　　　**Sect. 88-1**

David Dwight Wells was a secretary of the United States Embassy of London, and author of *Her Ladyship's Elephant*[4]*; His Lordship's Leopard: A Truthful Narration of Some Impossible Facts*[5]; and *Parlous Times: A Novel of Modern Diplomacy.*[6]

David Dwight Wells, born on April 22, 1868, was the son of the Honorable David Ames Wells (see his listing under Scientists) and Mary Sandford (Dwight) Wells.

In 1896, at the age of 28, Wells was the Secretary to Minister Bayard in the Court of St. James, London, England, a position which he held for two years.

In December of 1896, he married Marietta Harriet Ord, of England. Marietta, born on February 16, 1872, was the daughter of a London west end physician. They were married not quite four years.

David Dwight Wells died at the age of 32 on June 5, 1900. He had reportedly been ill about two weeks with typhoid fever and acute Bright's disease complications.

In November of 1901, Marietta H. Wells left America and returned to England.

4　*Her Ladyship's Elephant,* David Dwight Wells, New York, H. Holt and Company, 1898.
5　*His Lordship's Leopard: A Truthful Narration of Some Impossible Facts,* David Dwight Wells, New York, H. Holt and Company, 1900.
6　*Parlous Times: A Novel of Modern Diplomacy,* David Dwight Wells, New York, J.F. Taylor, and Company, 1900.

II.

Businessmen

Charles C. Alger (1809-1874)   Sect. 75-21

One of the most impressive and tallest monuments in the Yantic Cemetery is the Alger monument.

Charles Coffey Alger, also known as 'C.C.' Alger, was born the son of Levi Alger and Grace Coffey on July 4, 1809 in Vermont. Later the family moved to Orange County, New York.

On December 27, 1831, Charles Alger married Sarah Palmer of White Plains, New York. They had two children, Grace (ca. 1833-1899) who never married, and Charles (1836-1897). Sarah and Charles Alger were divorced in 1868, after 37 years of marriage. He soon married Marie Louise Molt, 30 years his junior. They had one daughter, Lucile Alger (1870-1936), who settled in Great Neck, Long Island in 1901. Lucile shared the estate with a friend, Miss Louise Nathalie Grace, and the estate was left to Miss Grace upon Lucile's death.

Alger held at least two patents for his iron works. He owned and operated the Stockbridge Iron Company in Stockbridge, Massachusetts from 1834 to 1850. Later, he and a partner built an iron furnace in Cold Spring, Putnam County, New York.

Charles Coffey Alger died in his summer home in New London on July 13, 1874. Marie Louise Molt Alger died while on a trip to Hanover, Germany on November 3, 1886 and was brought back to Norwich to be buried in the Yantic Cemetery.

These other two monuments in the Alger plot do not have names on them, but if one looks closely, initials can be seen that are present on their respective stones: CCA on the first, and MLA on the other, for Charles Coffey Alger and Marie Louise Alger.

Charles Bard (1827-1921)   Sect. 84-4

This stone caught my eye because of the lengthy family history listed on the memorial as well as the unique font.

Charles Bard was born in Canterbury, Connecticut on May 12, 1827, son of John and Mary (Foster) Bard. His wife Eliza Perkins (Daniels) Bard, daughter of Albert Daniels and Olive (Bolles) Daniels, was born on Christmas day in 1834. The memorial reads "Easterday" as her death date in 1870. Easter Sunday that year was April 17th. She left four children behind, ages 7, 6, 3 and 2.

Children:
- Charles Stedman Bard (1862-1873)
- Frank Nichols Bard (1864-1873)
- Albert Sprague Bard (1866-1963)
- Mary Foster (Bard) Williams (1868-1947), married Robert Williams

Charles Bard was a cashier at the Thames Bank, having been elected in 1857. The Thames Bank was incorporated in May of 1825 with its first president as William P. Greene.

In 1879, Bard is listed as the treasurer of the Thames Loan and Trust Company, which opened in 1870. By 1881, he had become the president.

15

In 1899, he is listed as the president of the First National Bank, located at 24 Shetucket Street. The First National Bank was incorporated in 1864.

He also served as president of the Norwich Savings Society from 1901 to 1913. The Norwich Savings Society incorporated in 1824, and moved to the corner of Main and Broadway on January 1, 1895.[1]

Eliza Bard died April 17, 1870. Charles Bard died January 14, 1921.

---

1 *Historical Sketch of Banking Norwich, Connecticut With Excerpts from Yesteryear,* by Severn T. Johanessen, 1976.

Enoch G. Bidwell (1829-1905)   Sect. 38-12

Enoch George Bidwell was a shoemaker, most specifically a maker of boots.
Born in Thompson, Connecticut on October 11, 1829, he was the son of Ira M.
Bidwell and Nancy (Church) Bidwell. Ira and Enoch had a shoe/boot business
downtown Norwich in the 1860's.

Enoch Bidwell was appointed postmaster in Norwich in 1870, and again in 1874.

The wife of Enoch Bidwell, Abby A. (Richards) Bidwell, was born in Connecticut
in 1834. Enoch and Abby Bidwell were married on November 16, 1852.

Children:
- William Francis Bidwell (1854-1916), buried in Dayville, Connecticut
- Carrie Estella Bidwell (1856-1939), married Frank L. Woodward (1856-1931)
- (unknown) Bidwell (1863-)
- Frederick Newton Bidwell (1864-1934), married Louise M. Pettit (1866-1951)

Enoch Bidwell died at the age of 75 on March 28, 1905. Abby Bidwell died
November 4, 1916.

Elijah A. Bill (1804-1884)   Sect. 29-10

If you make your way to the far back and center of the Yantic Cemetery, you will see what looks like a huge tree with the limbs cut off. The large granite stone is the memorial for E.A. Bill and his family. Stones of that type were built to indicate that all the branches of the family were lopped off. This is a very large and very stark visual reminder of just such history.

Elijah Abell Bill was born in Connecticut in 1804, the son of Phillip Bill (1767-1813) and Hannah Abell (1773-1859). He was a retail grocer in Norwich, Connecticut for many years. His business is listed as "groceries, wood ware, & c."[2] His store was located on Water Street in downtown Norwich. In 1840, he became president of the New London County Mutual Fire Insurance Company.

Later records would list him under woolen yarns and would indicate that he worked for the woolen manufacturer, Thames River Worsted Company, which was located at 48 Franklin Street in downtown Norwich.

His wife, Angelina Margaret (Hazard) Bill, was born in Rhode Island in 1810. They had a son who died young; a daughter who became a teacher and never married; and another daughter who, it seemed, never lived on her own. She lived with family members, and would live out the rest of her life at the Eliza Huntington Home.

Elijah A. Bill died in 1884. Angelina Bill died in 1891.

---

2 *Norwich Stedman Directory,* Price and Lee, 1861.

18

Lorenzo Blackstone (1819-1888)   Sect. 62-22

Lorenzo Blackstone, born June 21, 1819, was born and raised in Branford, Connecticut, the son of James Blackstone and Sarah Beach. His wife, Emily (Norton) Blackstone, was born July 19, 1820, the daughter of Asa Norton of Branford. In 1842, Lorenzo and Emily were married.

Shortly after they were married, they left America and moved to Liverpool, England to establish the sale of American goods in that country. He was the first to introduce Goodyear rubber to Great Britain. In 1846, he started selling the rubber goods from the Hayward Rubber Company of Colchester, Connecticut. He returned to Branford in 1855. By this time, his brothers-in-law, Henry, Timothy, and William Norton, had established themselves in business in Norwich, Connecticut and he moved to Norwich in 1857.

In 1859, after closing his business in England, he entered the cotton manufacturing business. He purchased a burned out mill, the former Blashfield Factory. He rebuilt it with a brick building and reopened it as the Attawaugan Mill. He would also purchase the Potokett Mill in Norwich (woolen mill) and was also director of the Ponemah Mills in the Taftville section of Norwich.

The Chelsea Savings Bank, located in Norwich, was incorporated in May 1858. Lorenzo Blackstone became its first president. In 1867, Blackstone became mayor of Norwich.

Children:
* James DeTrafford Blackstone (1846-1898)
* Harriet Blackstone
* Ella F. Blackstone, born in England, ca. 1853
* William N. Blackstone, born ca. 1856
* Louis Lorenzo Blackstone (1861-1892)

19

An interesting side note on the family: Lorenzo Blackstone was brother-in-law to Henry Bradley Plant, the man who brought the railroad to Tampa, Florida. Lorenzo Blackstone's sister, Ellen Elizabeth Blackstone, married Plant in 1843 in Branford, Connecticut. Ellen was the reason they moved to Florida. She was ill, and they felt a change of climate would be good for her. Ellen died in 1861 and is buried in her hometown of Branford.

In 1852, Henry and Ellen had a son named Morton. Morton Plant, nephew of Lorenzo Blackstone, would go on to establish the Shore-Line Railroad which opened in 1852 and extended from New Haven to New London. It would be eventually operated by the New York, New Hampshire and Hartford Railroad.

Henry Bradley Plant married again, and would carve out a dynasty that would include a railroad, steamboat and steamship enterprise in Florida. In 1873, Plant married Margaret Josephine Loughman, daughter of Martin Loughman. In 1891, Plant built the Tampa Bay Hotel at the cost of 3 million dollars, an unheard-of sum of money for a hotel. Major C.H. Smith, a popular humorist from the south also known as Bill Arp, was quoted in the *Indian Chieftain* newspaper, Vinita, Oklahoma on February 6, 1896. He described the Tampa Bay Hotel in this manner: "...on the banks of the Hillsborough River... has been erected the grandest structure that was ever designed for the purpose of a winter resort – Tampa Bay Hotel... massive, yet light and graceful in its perfect Moorish architecture..."

The building still stands, part of which is the Plant Museum in which one can experience the opulence of the era, from the tapestries on the wall to the furnishings, and rooms made to look as they did in the late 1800's. The other part of the former hotel is now used by the University of Tampa.

After contesting the will of his father who had originally left his fortune to his future great-grandchild, Morton and his stepmother would split a 22 million dollar estate, with Morton receiving two-thirds. With that money, he built the Plant Estate along with greenhouses, fabulous gardens, and the Branford House (designed by his wife) in the area of what is now known as Avery Point in Groton.

Lorenzo Blackstone died November 14, 1888. Emily Blackstone died October 1, 1896.

Lorenzo Blackstone, lithograph from
History of New London County.

Timothy B. Blackstone (1829-1900)   Sect. 124-8

The Blackstone memorial is an impressive and intricately carved granite stone.

Timothy Beach Blackstone was born in 1829 in Branford, Connecticut. He was the brother of Lorenzo Blackstone (also in this section). Timothy dropped out of school in 1847 due to ill health and began working with the New York and New Haven Railroad. In 1851, he moved to LaSalle, Illinois to work on the Illinois Central Railroad. He served as mayor (1854) in that city, and after that one year stint, he went back to the railroads. He became president of the Chicago and Alton Railroad, and helped to keep it from bankruptcy. After reorganization, he was president of the Board of Directors for the railroad. He refused his salary of $10,000 per year for all the years that he served as president.

In 1868, he married Isabella Farnsworth Norton. Born in Norwich on March 1, 1838, she was the daughter of Henry Norton. Henry, along with his brothers Asa and William, were all successful businessmen of Norwich, Connecticut.

"For thirty years Mr. Blackstone managed with consummate skill the affairs of this [Chicago and Alton Railroad], the most successful of all the great railroads of the Middle West. His policy was at once conservative and aggressive, a combination which made the Chicago and Alton railroad one of the best paying railroads of the United States. Its securities were eagerly sought after by the most conservative financiers and were recommended as one of the safest of endowment investments for charitable, educational or other public institutions."[3]

There is a street in downtown Chicago named for him. The Blackstone Hotel and Theatre, Chicago landmarks, are also named in his honor. The Blackstone Hotel sits on the site of his former mansion, and is pictured here.

Postcard of the Blackstone Hotel, Chicago, Illinois.

Blackstone served with the railroad until his resignation in 1899. He died of pneumonia on May 26, 1900. The funeral was held in Chicago, and his body transported for burial to Norwich, Connecticut.

Among the legacy he left behind were two libraries. The Chicago Public Library, Blackstone Branch, opened in 1904, was named in his honor. Branford, Connecticut also boasts a Blackstone Library, named in honor of his father, James Blackstone.

Isabella Norton Blackstone died September 30, 1928 in Chicago, Illinois and was brought back to Norwich to be buried with her husband.

---

3 *Biography of Timothy B. Blackstone*, by Ida Hinman M.S., M.A., published by Methodist Book Concern Press, New York, Cincinnati, Chicago, 1917.

Charles A. Burnham (1841-1883)   Sect. 122-49

Charles Abbott Burnham was born September 10, 1841 in the Sandwich Islands, now known as the Hawaiian Islands. His parents were in the islands helping build houses in a missionary effort. By 1850, his family had moved near his mother's family in Ellington, Connecticut. His father was Charles Burnham (1811-1893) of Massachusetts and his mother was Sarah Olivia Bliss (1810-1880) from Tolland, Connecticut. His mother Sarah died in San Francisco on November 19, 1880 while on vacation.

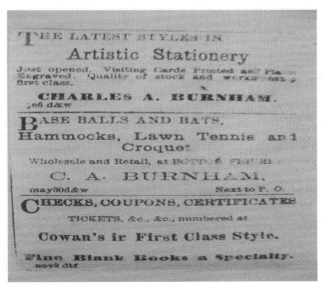

Charles Burnham moved to Norwich in 1864, and bought a "stationary, book binding, and paper hangings business"[4] downtown Norwich. The ad pictured here is from the *Norwich Bulletin*, 1883.

His first wife, Mary Foot Burt (born 1846), died in 1871 and he married Catherine (spelled

---

4 *Norwich Stedman Directory*, Price and Lee, 1861.

Katherine in some research material) Cook Lanman, daughter of Peter Lanman of Norwich. Charles and Catherine were married May 26, 1875.

Children of Charles and Catherine Burnham:
- Mabel Lanman Burnham Warner (1876-1950), married Fred Warner, died in San Diego, California
- C(K)atherine Cook Burnham (1878-)
- Charles Burnham (1880-)

Charles Burnham served faithfully as clerk for the Broadway Congregational Church for fifteen years.

In the obituary from the *Norwich Bulletin,* it was said of Charles Burnham that he was "enterprising, alert, honorable… warmhearted, modest, true… ."

Charles Burnham died July 4, 1883. His wife Catherine died in Tacoma Park, Maryland on February 23, 1930 and was buried on March 1, 1930 in the Yantic Cemetery.

William P. Greene (1795-1864)   Sect. 28

William Parkinson Greene, son of Gardiner and Elizabeth (Hubbard) Greene, was born September 26, 1795 in Boston. He graduated from Harvard in 1814 with a law degree, but his health was an issue and he did not pursue a career in law. He moved to Norwich in 1824, and became a partner in the Thames Manufacturer Company at the Falls. From 1825 to 1841, he served as President of the Thames Bank. In 1842, he was mayor of Norwich for one year, but poor health once again intervened.

William Greene was one of the incorporators of Norwich Free Academy which began in 1854, and he served on the board of trustees from 1857 to 1864. He also served as one of the original incorporators of the Norwich and Worcester Railroad. It is he for whom the Greenville section of Norwich is named.

His wife was Augusta Greene, born Augusta Elizabeth Borland in Boston on November 12, 1795. In 1859, she gave a house and grounds to be used by the principal of Norwich Free Academy.

Upon William's death it was said of him, "Seldom had the death of a citizen excited in the place so deep an interest and such profound regret."[5]

Augusta Greene died June 21, 1861. William Greene died June 18, 1864 at the age of 68.

---

5 *History of New London County,* p. 374.

Andrew Hagberg (1842-1930)   Sect. 115-50

Andrew Hagberg and his family lived in the Laurel Hill section of Norwich.
Hagberg was a tailor who worked with the Smith & Gilbert tailor shop for awhile,
as well as another area tailor for several years. He and his wife eventually owned
their own tailor shop on Main Street in downtown Norwich.

Andrew Hagberg was born in Sweden in 1842. His wife, Otillia A. Back (1843-
1917), was born in Sweden in 1843, the daughter of Dorothea W. Back, also of
Sweden.

Children:
*   Anna A. Hagberg (1866-1881), born in Sweden
*   John A. Hagberg (ca. 1868-), most likely born in Sweden
*   Charles A. Hagberg (1871-), born in Sweden, married Margaret, 3
    children listed to him
*   Gerda J.W. Hagberg (1873-), born in Sweden
*   Mary Hagberg (1875-), born in Sweden
*   Annie A. Hagberg (1882-), born in Connecticut, married John J. Young of
    Norwich

Hagberg became the vice-president of the Scandinavian Independent Political
Club, which was organized in 1900.

A. HAGBERG, TAILOR, 161 MAIN STREET.

Photograph from the *Norwich Evening Record,* p. 87.

Otillia Hagberg died March 16, 1917. Andrew Hagberg died March 7, 1930 at the age of 87.

Calvin L. Harwood (1844-1910)   Sect. 75-18

Calvin Luther Harwood served as mayor of Norwich from 1893 to 1896. He was also a merchant and businessman. He was a bookkeeper for Gurdon and Jones wholesale boot and shoe supplier, and eventually became a partner in the Lippett & Harwood wholesale grocery business (later known as Harwood & Company, and eventually Harwood, Bishop & Bidwell).

Calvin L. Harwood was born in Stafford, Connecticut in 1844, son of Francis Asbury Harwood and Clarissa Luther. He attended schools in Rhode Island and Massachusetts.

On September 26, 1865, he married Nellie A. White (also known as Ellen A.) of Hinsdale, New York, the daughter of John C. and Sarah B. (Potter) White. John C. White was from Northfield, Massachusetts. Calvin and Nellie Harwood moved to Norwich about 1868.

Children:
- Clara E. Harwood (1870-), married G.B. Dolbeare, bookkeeper at Norwich Savings Society
- Mary E. Harwood (1877-1878)
- Francis Harwood (1879-1956), worked as bookkeeper in father's business, married Mary Griswold (1878-1968)
- Alice W. Harwood (1879-1880), twin of Francis

Calvin Harwood died March 31, 1910. Ellen Harwood died February 27, 1925.

Henry H. Hazen (1820-1890)   Sect. 81-6

Henry H. Hazen was a stone mason who lived in the Preston area of Connecticut until he moved to Chicago, Illinois in 1888. Hazen and his wife lived only two years in the Chicago area when they passed away five months apart in 1890.

Henry Hyde Hazen was born in Franklin, Connecticut on July 28, 1820, the son of Henry and Sarah (Gifford) Hazen. His wife, Betsy Williams (Stanton) Hazen, was born in Franklin, Connecticut on January 1, 1825, the daughter of Rowland Stanton (1795-1886) and Hannah L. (Hewitt) Stanton (1805-1876).

Children:
- Rolena Hazen (1851-1854)
- Rocelia Hazen (1853-1865)
- Rowland Stanton Hazen (1855-1924)
- Marian E. Hazen Guttery Cleveland (1860-1939), first marriage to William P. Guttery of Chicago, Illinois in 1879; second marriage to Silas Ezra Cleveland of Chicago in 1904; she was proprietor of the Hazenhurst Hotel in Cedar Lake, Indiana from 1900 to 1922

Henry Hazen died in Chicago, Illinois on April 3, 1890. His wife, Betsy Hazen died five months later, on September 6, 1890 in Farm Ridge, Illinois (a small community about 150 miles south of Chicago). Both were brought back to Norwich to be buried in the Yantic Cemetery.

Jedediah Huntington (1791-1872)   Sect. 10-12

Jedediah Huntington was a successful mercantile businessman. For nearly 50 years, he was on the board of directors for the Norwich Bank. In addition, he helped build the railroad from Norwich to Worcester, and worked with that endeavor for many years.

Jedediah Huntington was born in Norwich to Levi Huntington and Ann Perkins on September 13, 1791. He lived about a decade in Troy, New York before returning to Norwich.

Jedediah Huntington,
History of New London County.

Eliza Huntington,
History of New London County.

In 1819, he married Eliza Wait, the daughter of Judge Marvin Wait of New London. They would live to celebrate their golden wedding anniversary in 1869. She died in 1871.

Their home for close to forty years was located on Washington Street. Upon his death in 1872, he carried out her wishes and bequeathed their house as a place for ladies who otherwise would have no home.

> "The Eliza Huntington Memorial Home for Respectable and Indigent Aged and Infirm Females was founded through the liberality of the late Jedediah Huntington, in furtherance of the desire of his deceased wife, Eliza, to render a public benefit to the community in which he lived."[6]

Eliza Huntington died March 19, 1871. Jedediah Huntington died March 23, 1872.

Postcard of the Eliza Huntington Home, Washington Street, Norwich, Connecticut.

---

6 *History of New London County,* p. 318.

Charles A. Kuebler (1852-1912)   Sect. 120-13

Charles A. Kuebler was born on September 1, 1852. He came to the United States from Germany in 1870. About that time, he began working as a stone cutter, eventually opening his own business and designing buildings as well as a number

of the beautiful monuments in the Yantic Cemetery, one of which was the Collins monument (pictured here).

His business was located on Franklin Street in the downtown area of Norwich. They used steam power for polishing the stones, and imported the stones from such places as Scotland, Sweden and Italy.

His wife Kate was born in Connecticut in 1850 of German parents. Records indicate they had four daughters: Henrietta, Isabelle, Julia and Mary.

Charles A. Kuebler died May 22, 1912. His wife Kate died December 24, 1928.

Picture from *Norwich Evening Record-Souvenir Edition.*

Moses Pierce (1808-1900)   Sect. 96-4

Moses Pierce earned his fortune in the mills. Born in Pawtucket, Rhode Island on July 3, 1808, he was the oldest son of Benjamin Bentley Pierce (1786-1839) and Susan Walker (1784-).

Pierce married Harriet Hathaway in Fall River, Massachusetts on November 24, 1831 at the age of 23. Harriet was born in Fall River, Massachusetts on April 13, 1813, the daughter of Simmons Hathaway (1781-1820) and Harriet Gardner (1785-1847).

Children of Moses and Harriet Pierce:
- Edwin Milman Pierce (1833-1861)
- Harriet A. Pierce (1836-1910)
- Sarah Walker Pierce (1838-1873)
- George Lyndon Pierce (1841-1852)
- Henry A. Pierce (1845-1846)
- Emily G. Pierce (1847-1921), married Thomas J. Wattles (born ca.1843)

Moses Pierce was one of the earliest advocates of the Tuskegee Institute and the education of blacks living in the south.

He also left a trust fund to the American Missionary Society of $100,000, which is outlined in the following article from the *New York Times*.

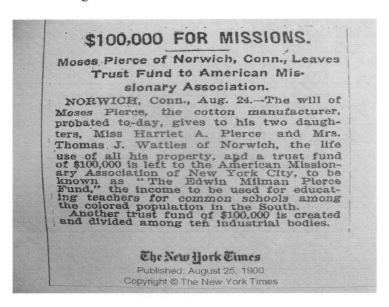

Moses Pierce donated his house (located in Norwichtown) plus ten acres of land to the United Workers for the purpose of establishing an orphanage, which eventually became the Rock Nook Children's Home.

Harriet Pierce died May 19, 1870. Moses Pierce died August 18, 1900.

The Pierce Family.

William P. Potter (1811-1887)   Sect. 124

William P. Potter has a most impressive metal monument. It is made of 'white bronze' which was really a zinc oxide. These memorials have stood the test of time, and most are in remarkable condition (see section on white bronze).

William P. Potter worked in the bleachery in the Greenville section of Norwich for a number of years, eventually becoming Superintendent.

He was born in Rhode Island on August 26, 1811. His wife Sarah D. Potter, born in 1812, was also born in Rhode Island.

Children:
- Charles H. Potter (1836-1898)
- William P. Potter, Jr. (1850-1901), worked in the bleachery
- Frank H. Potter (1856-1924), worked as invoice clerk (probably in bleachery)

William Potter died February 14, 1887. Sarah died December 18, 1904.

John Fox Slater (1815-1884)   Section 54-11

John Fox Slater was born March 4, 1815 in Slatersville, Rhode Island where his family owned the mills and the village. He was educated at the Plainfield Academy, as well as in Wrentham and Wilbraham, Massachusetts. He began working in his father's Hopeville, Connecticut mill at age 17 and took charge of the mill at age 21. In later years, he would be the sole owner of the mill in Jewett City, Connecticut. In 1842, he moved from Jewett City to Norwich.

His wife, Marianna Lanman Hubbard, was born February 15, 1824, the daughter of Eliza and Amos Hallan Hubbard.

Children:
- Marianna Hubbard (Slater) Bartlett (1845-1873); buried at Mt. Auburn, MA
- Josephine Eliza Slater (1848-1852)
- John Hubbard Slater (1851-1852)
- Elizabeth Bartlett Slater (1853-1855)
- John Fox Slater, Jr. (1855-1859)
- William Albert Slater (1857-1919)

John Fox Slater was known for his philanthropy. He helped to found the Norwich Free Academy, and endowed the school. The Slater Memorial Hall was donated by his son William (also in this chapter) and is named in honor of John Fox Slater. The Park Congregational Church, the congregation where he attended, also received an endowment.

In 1882, he donated $1,000,000, and the John F. Slater Fund for the Education of Freedmen was begun. It was to be used to assist in the industrial education of the blacks living in the south. Among the original trustees of the Slater Fund were Rutherford B. Hayes, Morrison R. Waite, William E. Dodge, Phillips Brooks, Daniel Coit Gilman, Morris Ketchum Jesup and the donor's son, William A. Slater.

John Fox Slater died May 7, 1884. His funeral was held at the Park Congregational Church in Norwich. Marianna Slater died February 19, 1889.

John Fox Slater, Memorial booklet, Norwich, Conn. 1885.

William A. Slater (1857-1919)   **Sect. 54-9**

William A. Slater was a businessman, mill owner, Harvard grad, philanthropist, world traveler, and founder of the Slater Memorial Museum as well as the Broadway Theater in Norwich. He also helped to establish the W.W. Backus Hospital in Norwich.

Born into wealth, Slater was a third-generation mill owner. His grandparents were John Slater (1776-1843) and wife Ruth Bucklin (1784-). John Slater, along with his brother Samuel Slater (1768-1835) who is often called the father of the industrial revolution, established the mill town of Slatersville, Rhode Island as well as a mill in Jewett City.

William Albert Slater was born on Christmas Day of 1857, the son of John Fox Slater and Marianna L. Slater. His wife, Ellen Burdett (Peck) Slater, was born in Worcester, Massachusetts on July 26, 1858.

Children:
* Eleanor Slater, born in February 1888 in Connecticut, first marriage to Boris de Struve of Russia; second marriage to E. Halsey Malone and they resided in New York City

- William A. Slater, Jr., born in Norwich, Connecticut in October 1890, died in 1962 in Montecito, California

Among Slater's gifts of philanthropy was the Slater Fund, which was established to help set up schools and educate the blacks living in the south. He also donated funds to help establish the YMCA in downtown Norwich.

Slater commissioned the Bath works company in Bath, Maine to build a steam-powered yacht which he named *Eleanor* for his young daughter. It was built in 1893-1894 and the staterooms were designed by Tiffany & Company. The cost for this state-of-the-art yacht, which was armed with Gatling guns and a "cannon or two," was $300,000.

Embarking on their journey on October 27, 1894, the family would take it on a "two-year tour of the world." One newspaper article called it a "floating palace." They were very fortunate on their trip. "Fair winds and following seas" certainly seemed to be a reality for them. While on a stop in the San Francisco harbor, William Slater was quoted as saying, "One strange feature... we have not been in a single storm. It has been lovely weather all the way around... we seem to miss all the heavy winds and ugly seas."[7]

During the Slater's Grand Tour of 1894 and 1895, one of their stops was in India. There they met up with the American missionary Robert Allen Humes, and invited his children on board the *Eleanor* for a birthday party for their daughter.

The family returned to New London on March 9, 1896 after their around-the-world tour and lived in Norwich until, in the early 1900's the family moved to Washington, D.C. By 1911, William A. Slater was somewhat of an invalid and divided his time between Washington, D.C. and Biarritz, France.[8] At this time, William A. Slater, Jr. had come back to Connecticut (Jewett City) to "learn the cotton manufacturing company from A to Z."[9]

The article goes on to say that daughter Eleanor Slater married a Russian diplomat named Boris de Struve of Petersburg, Russia in November of 1909. They were married at the Rue D'Arx, a Russian church in Paris, France. He died unexpectedly, after a short illness, in 1912. They had two children, a son and a daughter, Elana de Struve and Boris de Struve. Eleanor (Slater) de Struve returned to Washington upon the death of her husband and she would marry again, this time to Halsey Malone, an attorney in Washington, D.C. He was attending Georgetown University when he met her. They were married in St.

---

7 *San Francisco Chronicle*, July 23, 1895, p. 16.
8 *Ft. Wayne Sentinel*, Ft. Wayne, Indiana, December 11, 1911.
9 *San Francisco Chronicle*, July 23, 1895.

Patrick's Cathedral, Washington, D.C. on May 28, 1914, and eventually settled on Park Avenue, New York. One son Adrian was born in New York about 1915.

William Albert Slater died in Washington, D.C. on February 25, 1919. After William's death, Ellen continued to travel extensively. In September of that year, she reportedly traveled to France, England as well as Belgium.

William A. Slater, picture from the *Norwich The Rose of New England:
Prominent Personages* 1992 calendar, designed and printed by Franklin Impressions, Inc.

Edward A. Sterry (1811-1887)   Sect. 13-15

This beautiful lady is one of the more impressive monuments in the Yantic Cemetery.

At one time, Edward Sterry was a blacksmith. At a later date, he operated the Sterry Faucet Company, which he eventually turned over to his son, John. A New York newspaper article reported that there had been a fire in Sterry Faucet Company. The article begins "Between 1 & 2 o'clock Friday night, the building occupied by the Sterry Faucet Company and John A. Sterry manufacturer of faucets, stopcocks*, &c., at Norwich, Connecticut, was destroyed by an incendiary fire..." The article went on to say "The safe, with its books and papers, was saved; everything else was destroyed."[10] The Sterry Faucet Company was located in Norwichtown.

> [*a stopcock is a valve, tap, or faucet that regulates the flow of liquid or gas through a pipe, most specifically those located on the property boundary.]

Edward A. Sterry was born May 3, 1811 in Norwich, the son of John Sterry (1766-1823) and Rebecca Bromley (1776-1833). On May 15, 1833, Edward married Catherine Amelia Whittlesey. Catherine Whittlesey was born May 10,

---

10 *The New York Times,* July 6, 1873.

1810 in Saybrook, Connecticut, the daughter of John Tuttle Whittlesey and Betsy Whittlesey. The family attended the Park Congregational Church in Norwich.

Children:
- John Augustus Sterry (1834-1902), married Louisa Clymena Gould Westcott in New York, New York
- Annette Rebecca Sterry (1836-1912)
- George Edward Sterry (1838-1908)
- Frank William Sterry (1840-1886)
- Tully Whittlesey Sterry (1842-1876)
- Edward Augustus Sterry (1845-1845)
- Catherine Amelia Sterry (1847-1853)
- Caroline Augusta Sterry (1847-1924)

Catherine Whittlesey Sterry died July 17, 1874. Edward Sterry followed her in death August 27, 1887.

Alfred H. Vaughn (1828-1886)   Sect. 58-2

Alfred H. Vaughn was the superintendent of the Norwich Iron Foundry which was established in 1854. Among the items they manufactured were gears, pulleys, hangers, boxes, stoves, chimney caps, hitching posts and gas light posts.

A. H. Vaughn, as he was also known, was born in Rhode Island on February 26, 1828. His wife Eliza A. (Lamb) Vaughn was born in Connecticut on September 20, 1831, the daughter of Jefferson Lamb and Mary Crandall.

Stove located in one of the historical homes on the Norwichtown Green made by the Vaughn Foundry.

Another example of stove door made by the Vaughn Foundry Co., Norwich, Conn.

A.H. Vaughn died in Norwich on April 6, 1886. Eliza Vaughn died November 9, 1908.

Winslow T. Williams (ca. 1863-1930)   Sect. 23 (Evergreen Circle)

Winslow Tracy Williams was the third generation of Williams to own the Yantic woolen mill. His grandfather, Erastus Williams, had built the mill and his father,

E. Winslow Williams, had taken it over from his father. Winslow T. Williams had an older brother, Louis, who had died in 1888 and so it was that year that the mill was passed on to Winslow T. Williams.

Winslow T. Williams was born in Connecticut in 1863, the son of Erastus Winslow Williams and Elizabeth Dorr (Tracy) Williams. His wife, Florence P. Williams, was born circa 1864 in New York. Her father was from New York and her mother was from Italy.

Children:
- E. Winslow Williams (ca. 1892-1954), died in Lancaster, Pennsylvania
- Florence A. Williams (ca. 1898-1968), died in Lancaster, Pennsylvania, census listed her as a private secretary for a national bank

The mill burned in 1865, but was immediately rebuilt with granite to prevent such a recurrence (shown on postcard).

Early postcard of the Yantic Woolen Mill and mill houses, Yantic.

In 1908, Winslow Williams had a new stone bridge built across the Yantic River into the village of Yantic to replace the wooden one. The family estate in Yantic was known as Rockclyffe. In September of 1909, President William Howard Taft came to Norwich for the celebration of the 250th anniversary of the city and stayed with the Willliams family at their Rockclyffe estate. The new stone bridge was dedicated at that time.

There is an interesting side note about Winslow T. Williams. Apparently, he was quite a bicyclist and owned one of the early Expert Columbia bicycles (the type with the *huge* wheel in front, with a small wheel in the back). There is a reference to Williams, in which he is mentioned as a " 'League representative at Yantic,' has ridden a 56" nickled Expert, from '80 to '86, 5060 m., as measured by McDonnell and Butcher cyclometers."[11] (The 'league' may be in reference to the Wheeling Association which was started in 1880 to "fight for better roads and cycling clubs.")

Winslow T. Williams died in New York City on February 4, 1930. Florence P. Williams died December 7, 1952 at the age of 88 in Manhattan, New York.

---

11 *Ten Thousand Miles on a Bicycle,* by Karl Kron, New York, 1887, Chap. XXXI, p. 530, reprinted New York, E. Rosenblatt, 1982.

III.

Doctors

Dr. (Benjamin) Fordyce Barker (1819-1891)   Sect. 63-20

Benjamin Fordyce Barker was an obstetrician in Norwich, and gained his fame as a physician in New York. Born in Wilton, Maine in 1819, his father was John Barker, M.D., a distinguished doctor in Maine. His mother died of consumption when he was just a boy. After graduating from Bowdoin College in 1837, he went on to Harvard Medical College where he graduated in 1840 as well as from the Medical School in Maine in 1841. He then spent a year in Europe studying the various practices and hospitals of London, Edinburgh and Paris. He established a practice in Norwich, Connecticut in 1842 and continued that practice until 1850. His specialty was obstetrics. In 1843, he married Elizabeth Lee Dwight, daughter of James Sanford Dwight and Elizabeth Lee. They had one son, Fordyce Dwight Barker (1847-1893).

In 1845, he was elected Professor of Midwifery in the Medical School of Maine, but resigned after one course of lectures because it would require him to give up his practice. He was appointed Professor of Obstetrics in the New York Medical College in 1850. In 1855, he was elected physician of the Bellevue Hospital. Just two years later, he was elected the vice-president of the New York Academy of Medicine, and in 1859, he became president of the NY Medical Society. One year after that, he was appointed Professor of Obstetrics and the Diseases of Women and Children at the Bellevue Hospital Medical College. In 1864, he was elected chairman of the Section of Practical Medicine and Obstetrics. He also found time to be the president of the American Bible Society.

There is a narrative about Dr. Barker in "The Trial of Charles Guiteau: An Account" by Douglas Linder. In 1881, he testified for the prosecution at the trial of Charles Guiteau, the accused assassin of President Garfield.

In 1884, he was the head consulting physician of the brand new, state-of-the-art New York Cancer hospital. One of his patients at this time was Ulysses S. Grant, who suffered from cancer of the throat.

An interesting anecdote from his life: there was a book by James Wolvridge on midwifery, published in Dublin in 1670, which was touted as *the* book on midwifery. Dr. Fordyce Barker went to great lengths to try to obtain that book for the obstetrical society he was working with in New York City. He attempted to have the manuscript copied, having hired a man named Emile Bourgeaud (pronounced boor-joo) who was sought world-wide for his skills as a copyist. In April 1881, Bourgeaud returned to New York with the book only partly copied. Dr. Barker received a letter from him sometime later stating he would soon be going to Brazil, having received a commission from the Brazilian government as a copyist. Dr. Barker continued to track the man, finding out that he had returned to New York on a steamer, but he never saw the man or the book again. The obstetrical society did eventually acquire, not one, but *two* copies of the book.

Dr. Fordyce Barker died in 1891 in New York, and his body was brought back to Norwich to be buried. Elizabeth Barker died in Norwich on October 28, 1898.

Dr. Fordyce Barker,
One of New York's famous Physicians.

Dr. Samuel W. Fiske (1823-1902)   Sect. 130-18

Dr. Samuel W. Fiske had a very lucrative business as a "botanic physician and clairvoyant."[1] One observation on Dr. Fiske: "In 1869 Dr. S.W. Fiske, a 'self-styled astrologer, clairvoyant, and botanic physician,' claimed he could cure almost any disease and would make an examination of the sick 'for only a dollar.' "[2]

Samuel W. Fiske was born in Shelburn Falls, Massachusetts on December 29, 1823, the son of Alexander Fiske. Samuel's wife Lucina Pierce, daughter of David Pierce and Persis Cook, was born in Massachusetts on August 17, 1828. They were married circa 1848 in Thompson, Connecticut, and it was around 1872 that the family moved to Norwich.

Children:
*   Charles S. Fiske (1858-1921), married Ellen E. Mason (1859-1940)
*   Willie E. Fiske (ca. 1860-1882)
*   Persis M. (Fiske) Vars, married Washington Monroe Vars, who was listed as a sea captain

It was said of Dr. Fiske, a member of the Norwich Spiritual Union, that he had a "kindly disposition and was charitable."[3]

Dr. Fiske had suffered from rheumatism for several years before his death. He died January 4, 1902. Lucina Fiske followed him in death on August 6, 1908.

---

1 *Bicentennial Sketches of History and Nostalgia,* by Severn T. Johanessen, Thames Printing Company, 1976, p. 29.
2 Ibid.
3 Ibid.

Dr. Sidney L. Geer (1838-1906)   Sect. 87-3

Dr. Sidney Leonard Geer was a dentist in Norwich for about 50 years. Dr. Geer had studied under Dr. E. A. Cook, and eventually took over his practice when Dr. Cook moved to South America.

Sidney L. Geer was born in Scotland, Connecticut on September 17, 1838, the son of Jeptha Geer and Olive (Starkweather) Geer. At the age of 17, in 1855, he moved to Norwich to be under the apprenticeship of Dr. E. A. Cook. Dr. Geer maintained his practice until just before his death in 1906.

On July 20, 1865, he married Harriet L. Perry (known as Hattie) of Windham, Connecticut. She was the daughter of John B. Perry (1815-1870) and Harriet G. Perry (1813-).

Dr. Geer served on the board of commissioners for the water department of Norwich, and was chairman of the board for four years.

It was said of Dr. Geer that he "...was a man with the courage of his convictions and was held in the highest esteem by his many friends", and that he "possessed a pleasant and jovial disposition... ."[4]

---

4 *The Dental Cosmos: A Monthly Record of Dental Science,* edited by Edward C. Kirk, D.D.S, Sc. D., Volume XLIX-1907, p. 420.

Residence of Dr. Sidney Geer, Franklin Street, Norwich;
from Souvenir Edition, *Norwich Evening Record*.

Hattie Geer died March 15, 1898. Sidney Geer died April 18, 1906 "following a surgical operation at his home in the Geer block [on Broadway] ...in the sixty-eighth year of his age."[5]

5 Ibid., p. 421.

Dr. Charles Osgood (1808-1881)   Sect. 63

Dr. Charles Osgood was a physician and the son of a physician. His father, Erastus Osgood (ca.1779-1867), had been a physician in the local area for almost fifty years. His mother was Martha (Morgan) Osgood (1787-1876). Charles Osgood was born in Lebanon, Connecticut on February 13, 1808. He graduated from the Plainfield Academy and, desiring to follow in his fathers' footsteps, graduated with a medical degree from Yale College in 1833. He practiced medicine in Providence, Rhode Island as well as Monroe, Michigan.

In 1840, he returned to Norwich and established a drug business. He was also involved with a number of manufacturing businesses as well as banking. He established the Shetucket Bank in 1853 and served as its president. He was also one of the vice-presidents of the Norwich Savings Society.

Image of Charles Osgood, from *History of New London County.*

54

Not satisfied with just the above-mentioned businesses and enterprises, he was involved with the New London Mutual Fire Insurance Company and the Norwich Water-Power Company. Charles Osgood also aided in the founding of the Norwich Free Academy.

Osgood served as mayor of Norwich for one year, in 1876, but ill health caused him to resign.

It was said of Dr. Charles Osgood, he was a "good citizen, gentleman of superior culture, genial and social in manner, very popular with the masses... distinguished for his sterling integrity and business energy and tact."[6]

Children of Charles and Sarah Osgood:
- Thomas Larned Osgood (1840-1841)
- C. Henry Osgood (1842-1925), worked as a clerk in the drug store
- Frederic Larned Osgood (1849-1923), bookkeeper (probably for his father), chief of police in Norwich (1884-1885), married Eliza White (1848-1924)
- Cornelia Osgood (1856-), married Augustus C. Tyler

RESIDENCE OF C. H. OSGOOD, WASHINGTON STREET.

Residence of C.H. Osgood, corner Washington Street and Broad Street, Norwich.

Charles Osgood died March 18, 1881. His wife Sarah (Larned) Osgood followed him in death ten years later on September 11, 1891.

---

6 *The History of New London County,* p. 353.

IV.

Lawyers and Judges

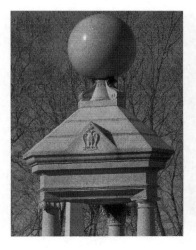 

Charles W. Carter (1838-1903)   Sect. 98-3

Charles W. Carter has a most unusual three-pillared stone. The Masonic eagle that graces one corner indicates he was a 33rd degree Mason.

Charles W. Carter was a lawyer and judge. He was born in Bristol, Connecticut on March 18, 1838. His first wife was Sarah (Greenman) Carter (1840-1886). After Sarah died in 1886, he married again, this time to Caroline Frances who was born in August 1838 in Johnston, Rhode Island. They made their home in Preston, Connecticut.

Honorable Charles W. Carter, Judge of Probate;
from *Souvenir Edition: Norwich Evening Record.*

Charles and his first wife, Sarah (Greenman) Carter had one child, Luther James Carter (1872-1908). Sarah died February 25, 1886.

His second wife, Caroline Frances Carter, died in 1902 and is buried in Killingly, Connecticut. Charles W. Carter died June 13, 1903.

Lafayette S. Foster (1806-1880)   Sect. 21-11

Lafayette Sabine Foster was Speaker of the House of Representatives in 1847, mayor of Norwich from 1851 to 1853, and U.S. Senator from 1854 to 1866. Foster was President Pro Tempore of the Senate in 1865 and, upon the death of President Lincoln, he became the acting Vice President of the United States. He was also professor of Law at Yale in 1868, justice of the Supreme Court of Connecticut from 1870 to 1876, and a benefactor of Yale, Norwich Free Academy as well as the Otis Library.

Lafayette Sabine Foster was born in Franklin, Connecticut on November 22, 1806, son of Daniel Foster and Welthea Almira Ladd. Foster was a descendant of Miles Standish through his grandmother, Hannah Standish.

Foster graduated from Brown University in 1828. After his graduation from Brown, he opened a law practice in Norwich.

He married twice. His first wife, Joanna Boylston Lanman, was born in Norwich on March 29, 1808. They married October 2, 1837 and she died April 11, 1859. The white marble stone on the left of Lafayette's is that of Joanna and depicts her and her small children in her arms as she is taken to heaven. All of their children died very young.

His second wife, whose stone is on the right of Lafayette's, was Martha P. Lyman, born in

1823 in Massachusetts, daughter of Honorable Jonathan H. Lyman, a lawyer from Northampton, Massachusetts.

Foster was one of those men who predicted the Civil War, and was in the forefront of restoration of the southern states after the Civil War.

After his service on the bench, he retired to Norwich and continued his law practice, where he was apparently very popular.

Lafayette S. Foster, image from *History of New London County.*

The obverse side of his tombstone reads: "A patriotic citizen, a wise counsellor, an eloquent advocate, a learned and incorruptible Judge, eminent and honored in the Senate of the United States, in all his distinguished service to his country and to mankind he counted no dignity so high as that of a disciple of JESUS CHRIST, no possession so dear as the favor of GOD."

His house became a part of the Norwich Free Academy, and that building now includes the school library.

Lafayette Foster died in Norwich on September 19, 1880. Martha Foster died January 20, 1903.

V.

Mariners

Captain Chester Hillard (1815-1868)   Sect. 48-8

Buried in the Yantic Cemetery is a fellow by the name of Captain Chester Hillard. His epitaph reads "the only surviving passenger of the illfated Lexington." In the 1830's, the steamship *Lexington* sailed from New York to Massachusetts with stops at Providence, Rhode Island as well as Stonington, Connecticut. She had the reputation of being the fastest vessel from New York to Boston. Hillard was a steamboat captain, but was not part of the crew that night and was just traveling on the *Lexington*.

On one particular cold day, January 13, 1840, the *Lexington* caught fire just four miles off the coast of Long Island. She was carrying 143 passengers and crew, and 150 bales of cotton. Sparks from the coal-driven engines set the bales on fire, which were stored in close proximity to the smokestacks.

The regular captain of the ship, Jacob Vanderbilt, was home sick with a cold. The ship's captain that night was Captain George Child. At 7:30 p.m., flames could be seen. Captain Child attempted to bring her a little closer to shore, but by now the fire had ravaged the steering mechanism, burning the lines through from rudder to wheelhouse. Crew members were forced out of the engine room before they could shut her down. The ship was going full speed, but out of control.

They attempted to launch the few lifeboats they had on board the ship. With the ship at full tilt, the lifeboats were churned into the water, spilling their passengers into the freezing water. Some of the cotton bales were thrown over, and some managed to climb onto them.

By 3 a.m., the ship was gone. It had sunk into the Long Island Sound. Only 4 people managed to survive. One man, Second Mate David Crowley managed to climb onto a bale of cotton and stay warm. He floated for 48 hours until he washed ashore, showing up on someone's doorstep where he stayed until he was strong enough to travel back home. It is said that he kept that bale of cotton in his Providence, Rhode Island home until the Civil War, when it was eventually sold for the war effort.

Chester Hillard managed to climb onto a plank and was rescued the next afternoon. Besides Hillard and David Crowley, only two other crew members survived, Captain Stephen Manchester and Charles Smith.

The ship still lies in Long Island Sound. They tried to raise it in 1842, only to have it break up and go to 130 feet. One man, Adolphus Harnden, was carrying $20,000 in silver coins, and some $50,000 in bank notes. The box holding the silver was dumped onto the deck, and used as a floating device. A 30 pound mass of silver was eventually salvaged from the ship.

Chester Hillard was born in Preston, Connecticut on November 26, 1815, the son of Moses and Sally Hillard. He was married to Julia A. (Barker) Hillard, who was born on November 5, 1818.

Chester Hillard lived another twenty-eight years after the *Lexington* event, and died on March 21, 1868. Julia Hillard died December 17, 1875.

Captain William R. Hull (ca. 1812-1849)   Sect. 9

The stone memorial reads "Capt. William R. Hull, of the ship *Alibree,* Died on the Pacific Ocean, Lat 11 South, Lon 121 West, January 21, 1849, Aged 37 years." Latitude of 11 degrees south and longitude of 121 degrees west would have placed the ship about 1,100 km (approximately 700 miles) west and 30 degrees south of the Galapagos Islands, directly in the middle of the Pacific Ocean.

The *Alibree* was a 373 ton bark used in the whaling industry, listed with the "Agents I&W.P. Randall." Apparently, this was the last trek of the *Alibree.* The last voyage listed for her was from "June of 1847-April of 1849."[1]

Captain Hull had served on the *Armata* out of New London, Connecticut (another whaling vessel which plied the waters of the Indian Ocean), as well as the *Alibree* (Pacific Ocean and Northwest coast of America) out of Mystic, Connecticut.

Whaling was a dangerous business. One article reads, "...we find the names of no less than twenty-three persons reported, who have been killed by whales within a short period."[2] This fate also befell Captain Luke J. Avery of Mystic, Connecticut, also on board the *Alibree,* who was killed two years prior on August 16, 1847.

William R. Hull died on January 21, 1849, and was most likely buried at sea.

---

1 *Groton, Conn. 1705-1905*, by Charles R. Stark, published by The Palmer Press, 1922, p. 353.
2 *Public Ledger,* Philadelphia, Pennsylvania, March 18, 1847, reprinted from the *New York Sun.*

Captain John Parker (1772-1819)   Sect. 22-20

Captain John Parker was an American sea captain until after the War of 1812, at which time he went to Mexico to be a part of the Mexican Navy while that country was at war. He reached the rank of Commodore and was the captain of the brigantine *Mexican Congress* when he died of a fever on board in the Bay of Honduras and was buried ashore May 27, 1819. The Mexican government gave land grants to his family in appreciation for his service, but they were never claimed.

John Parker was born March 10, 1772. His wife, Sarah (Fitch) Parker, was born August 10, 1771. They were married in 1802 in Norwich, Connecticut.

Following are two references that were found of the *Mexican Congress* from newspapers of that era.

"Latest from Amelia Island [Florida]. It was reported that he [Commodore Aury] was fitting out an expedition consisting of the brigs *Mexican Congress, Republican* (formerly the *Morgina), America Free,* and four schooners… their destinations unknown."[3]

"The Mexican brig *Mexican Congress,* was to sail from Tybee Light on Sunday last."[4]   (The Tybee Light referred to is the Tybee lighthouse on the Savannah River, Tybee Island, Georgia).

Captain John Parker died May 27, 1819. Sarah Parker died November 14, 1847.

---

3 *The Evening Post,* New York, New York, dated January 19, 1818.
4 *The Evening Post,* New York, New York, dated April 2, 1818.

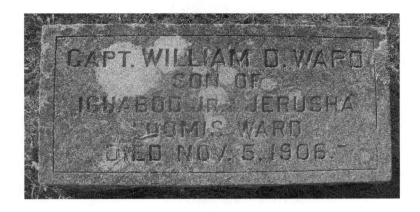

Captain William D. Ward (1827-1906)   Sect. 40-2

Captain William Dygert Ward, steamship captain, was born in Connecticut in February 1827, the son of Icabod Ward, Jr. and Jerusha Bancroft (Loomis) Ward. The family lived on Mt. Pleasant Street, which gave a great view of the Thames River.

William Ward received his Seaman's Protection Certificate in 1844. This would be his life for the next 55 years. Ward's first ship he served aboard was the clipper ship *Quebec* with Captain Frederick H. Hebard. He would serve on the schooners *Hudson, William P. Williams* and the *Joseph Guest.* Among the ships he served as captain were the *City of Lawrence, City of New London, City of New York,* and the *City of Boston.* The *City of Boston* was an iron-hulled steamship, part of the Inman Line that ran out of Halifax, Nova Scotia to Liverpool, England. Built in 1864, her maiden voyage was in February 1865 from Liverpool to New York. In 1870, with Captain Halcrow at the helm, she was lost with all 191 on board in the North Atlantic and no trace of her was ever found.

Angeline (Ann) Harvey (Smith), wife of William D. Ward, was born April 22, 1831 in Preston, Connecticut, the daughter of Charles Granderson Smith (1803-1864) and Elizabeth Billings Standish (1805-1883).

Children:
- Mary E. Ward (ca. 1852-)
- Emma Ward (1852-1920), in 1880 she was teaching school in Norwich
- Jesse H. Ward (ca. 1857-1867)
- Ann Ward (1861-)
- William D. Ward (1863-1930)
- Nathan Ward (b. ca. 1866)
- Martha Ward (1866-1921)
- Lester Ward (ca. 1869-1870)

- Sybil Blossom Ward (1870-1953)
- Gertrude Ward (ca. 1874-1947), school teacher at the Mt. Pleasant School, Norwich

Angeline Ward died January 13, 1899. William Dygert Ward died November 5, 1906 in Norwich.

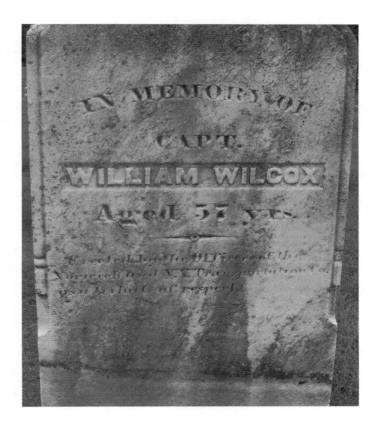

Captain William A. Wilcox (1812-1869)   Sect. 10-11

Captain William A. Wilcox was a steamboat captain who died by his own hand on board the steamship *City of Boston* in April 1869. The epitaph reads "Erected by the Officers of the Norwich and N.Y. Transportation Co. as a tribute of respect."

William Wilcox was born in Connecticut in 1812. His wife Nancy Wilcox was born circa 1820 in Connecticut.

Children:
* George Wilcox, b. ca. 1842
* Elizabeth Wilcox, b. ca. 1846
* Charles Wilcox, b. ca. 1848
* Jane Wilcox, b. ca. 1850, married Henry W. Lester
* Lucy Wilcox, b. ca. 1855

From an early age, William Wilcox showed an interest in sailing. He began his career on steamboats in 1836 as a wheelsman on the *Norwich* piloted by Captain W.W. Coit. In 1838, he served as pilot on the Connecticut River between Hartford and Saybrook. He served on the *Knickerbocker;* was Captain of the

71

Worcester, the *Cleopatra,* the *Connecticut;* and served as the Captain of *City of Boston* from 1860 to 1866, and the *City of Lawrence* until his retirement in 1867.

Wilcox retired to North Stonington. According to his obituary, "Captain Wilcox was widely known as one of the best steamboat men on Long Island Sound... he met not with a single accident, and there was no officer more popular than he..."[5]

On Monday, April 12, 1869, he told his daughter, Jane Lester, that he was going to New York, giving her the keys to his trunk, his gold watch and his eyeglasses. His son-in-law, Henry Lester, took him to the depot. All indications were that he was in good spirits. Tuesday morning word was received that Captain Wilcox was missing. His hat and cane were found on deck. When his body was discovered in Long Island Sound, there was a bullet hole in his temple. It is believed he "placed himself in a position that he would fall into the water... put the pistol to his head and discharged it."[6]

Captain William Wilcox was laid to rest on April 16, 1869. His wife Nancy died at the age of 54 on July 7, 1884.

---

5 *Norwich Bulletin,* April 13, 1869.
6 Ibid.

VI.

Mausoleums

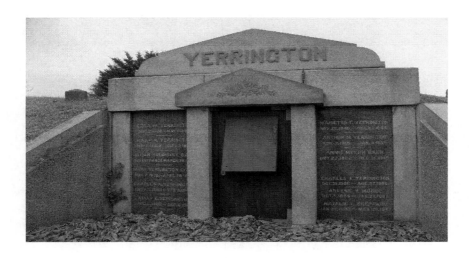

Allen T. Baer (1864-1900)   Yerrington Tomb

Allen Trumbull Baer was a member of the Yerrington family, and is one of those buried in the Yerrington mausoleum (see another Yerrington later in this chapter). He was the son-in-law of Ezra and Mary Yerrington, and husband of Annie Meech Baer.

Allen T. Baer was born in South Bend, Indiana on May 11, 1864. In 1885, he worked as a telegraph operator of the Western Union Telegraph Company.[1] In 1888, he was listed as an "Assoc. Press telegraph operator"[2] and according to his obituary, he was an expert at it.

On November 26, 1888, he married Anne (Annie) Meech Yerrington, the daughter of Ezra W. Yerrington and Mary (Huntington) Yerrington. Anne was born October 22, 1862.

Allen Baer wrote articles for various papers, and in 1889, he became a reporter for the *New York Sun.* By 1893, he had moved to the *New York Herald.* In 1897, he was the managing editor of the *Evening Telegram* until ill health prevented him from continuing. In 1899, he went abroad and worked for the Paris edition of the *New York Herald.*

On March 28, 1900, Baer died in Paris of the influenza and his body was shipped back to Connecticut to be buried with his wife's family. He left behind a wife and a seven year-old son, Sterling.

Anne Meech Baer died in Mamaroneck, New York on December 31, 1943. Their son, Sterling Baer, died in North Canaan, Connecticut on November 9, 1974.

---

1 *Norwich Stedman Directory,* 1885.
2 *Norwich Stedman Directory,* 1888.

Gurdon Chapman (1797-1864)   Sect. 103

Gurdon Chapman and his two wives are buried in the family tomb. Gurdon Chapman was born in North Stonington, Connecticut on April 10, 1792 but moved to Norwich at an early age. He worked for Hyde, Smith and Company, which dealt in grain and flour, etc.

He didn't have much in the way of formal education, but he studied on his own. He served as mayor of Norwich from 1843 to 1845, and "he was also frequently called to responsible positions in the affairs of the town." He was "a clear thinker, forcible and fluent public speaker..." and was "highly respected and esteemed for his integrity, the kindness of his heart, and the soundness of his judgment..."[3]

His first wife, Elizabeth (Phillips) Chapman, also from North Stonington, was born August 1, 1794. She died March 9, 1850.

Gurdon Chapman died February 29, 1864 (leap year). His second wife, Mary Ann (Moore) Chapman, died January 31, 1892.

---

3 *History of New London County, Connecticut*, p. 373.

William C. Robinson (1834-1911)   Mausoleum

William Callyhan Robinson was a lawyer as well as a theologian. Robinson
graduated from Dartmouth College in 1854 and from the Theological Seminary of
the Protestant Episcopal Church in 1857. He served as pastor of the Episcopal
church in Pittston, Pennsylvania for two years and served in Scranton,
Pennsylvania from 1859 to 1862. Robinson left his pastorate in 1862 and joined
the Catholic Church a year later. He was admitted to the legal bar in 1864. He
became a lecturer and professor of law at Yale University and served in that
capacity from 1869 to 1895.[4] He served for two years as judge of the City Court
as well as the Court of Common Pleas in New Haven, Connecticut, and was a
member of the Legislature.

In 1879, Dartmouth bestowed upon him an LL.D. degree, and in 1881 he received
his M.A. from Yale. It was said of him, "His thorough knowledge of law made
him eminent as a teacher and enabled him to render important service to the
Church."[5] From 1895 until his death in 1911, he was a professor in the Catholic
University of America in Washington, D.C. There he organized the School of

---

4 Information from *Catholic Encyclopedia;* Robert Appleton Company, New York, New York,
Vol. 15, 1912, "William Callyhan Robinson."
5 Ibid.

Social Sciences. He served as Dean of the School of Law until his death in Washington, D.C.

William Callyhan Robinson was born in Norwich, the son of John Adams Robinson (1809-1888) and Mary Elizabeth (Callyhan) Robinson. His first wife was Anna Elizabeth Haviland, born in Boston, Massachusetts on December 23, 1830. She married William, by then a judge, in Manhattan, New York on July 2, 1857. She died January 3, 1889 in New Haven, Connecticut. Five children are listed with this union: Mary, Osmyn, Philip, George and Paul.

Robinson married a second time on March 31, 1891. His wife Ultima was born in Cuba in 1868. They had 4 children: Thomas R. (1892-1957); Richard W. (1893-); a daughter Ultima (1895-1956); and a son John Andrew (1902-1904).

Ultima Robinson died in Liberty, New York on September 1, 1905. William C. Robinson died in Washington, D.C. on November 6, 1911. Both are buried in the mausoleum, along with several other family members.

Ezra W. Yerrington (1828-1890)   Mausoleum

Ezra Witter Yerrington was born in Norwich, Connecticut on August 17, 1828, the son of Joseph Parke Yerrington and Mary Parke Meech. His wife, Mary Huntington Yerrington, was born May 24, 1826, the daughter of Isaac (1775-1842) and Hannah Huntington (1786-1838). Ezra and Mary were married in 1847 in Bozrah, Connecticut.

E.W. Yerrington, as his business was known, was a merchant in Norwich for many years. He is listed as selling "pianos and organs."[6] Later on, he also included "paper hangings, carpets, rugs."[7] He continued his business until shortly before his death in 1890.

Children:
- Charles A. Yerrington (1858-1943)
- Annie Meech Yerrington Baer (1862-1943)

Ezra Yerrington died May 1, 1890 at the age of 61. His wife, Mary H. Yerrington died September 3, 1913.

---

6 *Norwich Stedman Directory*, 1867.
7 *Norwich Stedman Directory*, 1880.

Charles Young (1821-1897)   **Mausoleum**

A remarkable statue graces the door of the Young tomb.

Charles Young and his wife were both born in Bavaria, Germany. Charles was born in 1821 and Phillipena was born in 1825.

Much of the following has been gleaned from research done by local cemetery historian David Oat. Charles Young served in the German army from about 1843 to 1849 as a Bavarian officer. Bavaria was defeated in the Prussian and Bavarian war and Young had to flee for his life. First landing in New York, the couple made their way to Norwich just two days later. When Charles and Phillipena came to the United States, they had only been married a few weeks.

In Norwich, Charles worked for Vaughn's Foundry as a moulder. Phillipena became quite well known as a seamstress and dressmaker. Through her enterprising skills, they were able to save money allowing them to purchase the corner building at Main and Franklin Streets in downtown Norwich. They were eventually able to purchase other surrounding buildings and the block became known as Young's block.

In 1870, Charles is listed as a "saloon keeper."[8] In 1871, the couple purchased the home at 34 East Town Street which had belonged to Dr. William W. Cutter and comprised seven acres. It is the property most commonly known today as the Samuel Huntington homestead. The Youngs built greenhouses and operated a fruit and flower farm.

---

8 *Norwich Stedman Directory,* Price and Lee, 1870.

The couple only had one child, a daughter Josephine born in Connecticut about 1863 who died at just two days old.

As a widow, Phillipena continued to increase the family fortune. It is said she remained alert, without even a pair of spectacles, and would often travel to New York on business.

Charles Young died May 27, 1897 and was buried in a beautiful vault his wife had built for him. Phillipena Young died September 13, 1916 at the age of 91.

VII.

Military

Rear Admirals Lanman and Carr   Sect. 122

It is quite an accomplishment to have *one* person in a family to achieve the rank of Rear Admiral. It is quite rare to have *two* of that rank in the same family. Alice Blanche Lanman (1864-1949) has the distinction of being the daughter of one Rear Admiral, and the wife of another. Her father was Rear Admiral Joseph Lanman. Her husband was Rear Admiral Clarence Carr. The two distinguished admirals are buried next to each other.

Rear Admiral Joseph Lanman (1811-1872)

Joseph Lanman was born in Norwich, Connecticut on July 18, 1811. In January 1825, he was appointed midshipman when he was not quite 14 years of age. Among the ships he served aboard were the *Macedonian,* the *Peacock* (a sloop) and the schooner *Dolphin.* In 1835, Lanman received his commission as lieutenant where he served on the *Vincennes.* His travels took him to the South Sea Islands and the Mediterranean. He was stationed in California in 1848 when they discovered gold. In 1858, he was given command of the United States Steamer *Michigan,* which patrolled the Great Lakes. In 1861, at the outbreak of the Civil War, he was sent to Mare Island, California where he was ordnance officer. In 1862, he commanded the *Saranac,* stationed at Panama, to protect the Isthmus railway and for the safety of the passengers. Lanman commanded the frigate *Minnesota* from 1864 to 1865. He was present at the two attacks on Fort Fisher, the second of which he was chosen to lead the forces for the attack. The combined attack of land and sea forces resulted in the capture of Fort Fisher. In

October 1865, Lanman was given command of the North Atlantic Squadron. In October 1867, he took command of the Portsmouth, New Hampshire Navy Yard, and in December of that year, he received his commission as Rear Admiral. He was cruising off the coast of Brazil with the South Atlantic Squadron in 1869.

Rear Admiral Lanman's tombstone states that he died in 1872, but all indications are that he died on March 13, 1874. According to an article from *The Leavenworth Times*, Leavenworth, Kansas, dated July 25, 1872, Rear Admiral Joseph Lanman "lately commanding the South American Fleet, has been placed on the retired list...". An article from an Indianapolis newspaper, dated March 14, 1874, states that "Rear Admiral Joseph Lanman, of the U.S. Navy died at his residence in Norwich, Connecticut yesterday [March 13, 1874], age 63."

Rear Admiral Clarence Alfred Carr (1856-1930)

Clarence Alfred Carr was born in Mosiertown, Pennsylvania on July 26, 1856. He graduated from the United States Naval Academy in 1879 and from Stevens Institute of Technology in Hoboken, New Jersey in 1884 with a degree as a marine engineer. His career in the Navy began in 1881 as an assistant engineer. In 1898, he became chief engineer. That same year, on October 19, he married Alice Blanche Lanman, daughter of Rear Admiral Joseph Lanman. During World War I, Carr served as the engineering officer of the Philadelphia Navy Yard. He would continue to serve the Navy for 40 years until his retirement in 1921, having achieved the rank of rear admiral on September 26, 1919.

After his retirement, he and his wife made their home on Montauk Avenue in New London, Connecticut, and he died there on March 9, 1930. 'Blanche' Lanman Carr died December 8, 1949.

Civil War

William Appleton Aiken (1833-1929)   Sect. 50-10

William Appleton Aiken, son of John Aiken, was born in Vermont on April 18, 1833. Among the private schools he attended was the Phillips Academy in Andover, Massachusetts. Aiken was the nephew of President Franklin Pierce.

His wife was Eliza Coit (Buckingham) Aiken, born in Connecticut on December 7, 1838, the daughter of William Buckingham, Governor of Connecticut, and Eliza (Ripley) Buckingham. William and Eliza were married in Norwich on August 28, 1861.

Children listed to them:
- Eliza Aiken (circa 1862-1933)
- William B. Aiken, born January 1864, died February 21, 1903 at age 39
- Mary A. Aiken (April 1866-1959)
- Jane M. Aiken (1867-1949)
- Alfred L. Aiken, born July 1870, died December 3, 1946 in New York City
- John Aiken (1871-1893)
- Edith M. Aiken (1873-1898)

At the outbreak of the Civil War, Aiken joined the Navy and took part in the battle at Hilton Head, South Carolina. He became Quartermaster General of the state of Connecticut, visiting his state regiments in the field. He met with Winfred Scott as well as President Lincoln. When President Lincoln was assassinated, it was he,

Governor William Buckingham and Senator Lafayette Foster that traveled to the White House to show their support for the new administration.

After the war, Aiken became the president of the Norwich Nickel and Brass Company of Norwich, Connecticut.

He served as a Trustee of the Otis Library for almost 40 years, resigning in December of 1907.

Elizabeth died at the age of 85 on July 31, 1924. William A. Aiken died November 7, 1929 at the age of 96.

Captain William A. Berry (1838-1864)   Sect. 76-18

Captain William A. Berry: "a gallant soldier, faithful to his adopted country."[1] Berry died while serving in the Civil War at Petersburg, Virginia in June 1864.

William A. Berry was born in England in 1838. He had begun living in the Greenville section of Norwich about the time the war broke out. The first company raised in Norwich was the Buckingham Rifles, and Berry was the first to enlist in that company where he was commissioned a 2nd Lieutenant. Later he would join Captain Maguire's company of the 2nd New York Light Artillery, where he was promoted to captain. He was killed near Petersburg, Virginia on June 18, 1864. Originally buried on the battlefield, he was brought back to Norwich by a fellow soldier, Captain Thomas Scott.

Captain William A. Berry died on June 18, 1864 and was re-interred in the Yantic Cemetery on November 3, 1864.

---

1 *History of Norwich,* p. 681.

Frank Stuart Bond (1830-1912)   **Sect. 83**

Frank Stuart Bond was born in Sturbridge, Massachusetts in 1830, the son of Reverend Alvan Bond (found in another section of this book) and his wife Sarah (Richardson) Bond.

Frank Bond served in the Civil War as a commissioned officer. In March of 1862, he was commissioned an officer and promoted to Full 1st Lieutenant in Company B, Connecticut 10th Infantry Regiment. Commissioned an officer in the U.S. Volunteers Aide-de-Camp on March 11, 1863, he was promoted to Major. He was mustered out on November 18, 1864.

Bond had begun working for the railroad in 1849, and except for his time served in the war, he would be involved with the railroad until his retirement in 1902. According to his online biography, "He entered the railway service in 1849; to 1851 in the office of the treasurer of the Norwich & Worcester Railroad Company; 1851 to 1856, secretary Cincinnati, Hamilton & Dayton Railroad Company; 1857 to 1861, secretary and treasurer Auburn & Allentown Railroad Company and Schuylkill & Susquehanna Railroad Company; 1862 to 1864, served in the army, United States Volunteers; 1865 to 1867, not in active business; 1868 to 1873, vice-president Missouri, Kansas & Texas Railway Company; 1873 to 1881, vice-president Texas & Pacific Railway Company; 1881 to 1882, president Philadelphia & Reading Railroad Company; 1884 to 1886, president of five associated railways, the Cincinnati, New Orleans & Texas Pacific Railway Company, Alabama Great Southern Railroad Company, New Orleans & Northeastern Railroad Company, Vicksburg & Meridian Railroad Company, and Vicksburg, Shreveport & Pacific Railroad Company; since 1886, vice-president Chicago, Milwaukee & St. Paul Railway Company; resident in New York City."[2]

He retired to New London. He died in Jekyll Island, Georgia (a popular resort of that era) on February 26, 1912 and was buried on March 1, 1912.

---

2 http://www.all-biographies.com/soldiers/frank_stuart_bond.htm

William A. Buckingham (1804-1875)   Sect. 50-22

William A. Buckingham was a merchant and manufacturer, as well as mayor of Norwich, Governor of Connecticut, Senator of the United States and a revered public official. William A. Buckingham was born in Lebanon, Connecticut on May 28, 1804, the son of Samuel Buckingham (1770-1850) and Joanna (Mattson) Buckingham (1777-1846).

Buckingham was educated at the local public schools and labored on the farm during vacations. He taught one year of school, then became a merchant working as a clerk with a mercantile firm in Norwich. At the age of 23, he opened his own store in Norwich.

On September 27, 1830, he married Eliza Ripley of Norwich. They had one daughter, Eliza Coit Buckingham (1838-1924) who married William A. Aiken (another subject earlier in this chapter); and a son, William Ripley Buckingham (1836-1838).

He "soon added manufacturing to his mercantile pursuits..." His family was involved in the Hayward Rubber Company. In business and in his personal life, he was noted for his "...stern integrity and grandeur of character..."[3]

---

3 *History of New London County,* Philadelphia, 1882, p. 349.

Buckingham served as mayor of Norwich, Connecticut from 1849 to 1850, and again from 1856 to 1857. In 1858, he ran as a Republican and was elected Governor of Connecticut. "For eight consecutive years he was re-elected to that exalted and honorable position...." It was, in the eyes of some, "...the most eventful period of American history."[4] His last term as Governor ended in 1866.

In 1868, he was elected Senator, and for six years he was "a much-revered, able, efficient, and highly-respected member of that august body."[5]

Image of Wm. Buckingham from *History of New London County.*

Early postcard of former Buckingham residence, now the Buckingham Memorial, downtown Norwich.

Eliza (Ripley) Buckingham died April 19, 1868.

By 1874, Buckingham's health was beginning to fail. It is said that his last days were "peaceful and serene."[6] William A. Buckingham died on February 5, 1875.

---

4   Ibid, p. 349.
5   Ibid.
6   Ibid.

Lucius T. Bushnell (1832-1905)   **Sect. 17**

Lucius T. Bushnell was born in Norwich in March 1832, the son of Theron and Seria Bushnell. His father, Theron, was a machinist in Norwich. Lucius, in the 1900 census report, is listed as a carriage painter living in Preston with his wife Frances. Frances A. Bushnell was born in Norwich in 1835.

During the Civil War, Bushnell served aboard the *U.S.S. Daylight*, a screw-type steam powered gunboat. This ship was used by the Union Navy to blockade the south from trading with other countries. Built in 1859, she was put to use in 1861 in Virginia and along the Atlantic coast, as far south as Wilmington, North Carolina.

The *U.S.S. Daylight* was part of the bombardment of Fort Macon, North Carolina on April 25 to 26, 1862. She was also part of the attack on Fort Fisher in November of that year. The ship was decommissioned May 24, 1865, and sold in October that same year.

Lucius Bushnell died on August 7, 1905. Frances Bushnell died in Taunton, Massachusetts on May 13, 1917.

William G. Ely, Brigadier General (1836-1906)   Sect. 53-1

Brigadier General William G. Ely was a businessman, civil engineer and prominent Civil War general. He was born in West Killingly, Connecticut on December 12, 1836, the son of Jesse Ely (1807-1879) and Harriet Grosvenor Ely (1813-1875). William Ely graduated from Brown University as a civil engineer and completed his education in France as well as in Germany.

William Ely married Augusta Elizabeth Greene on January 9, 1865. Augusta Greene was born April 6, 1834 in Norwich. She was the daughter of William Parkinson Greene (1795-1864) and Augusta Elizabeth (Borland) Greene (1795-1861).

Children:
- William J. Ely
- Anna Lloyd Ely (1866-1960)
- Anna G. Ely (1868-)
- William Grosvenor Ely (1869-1936)

At the outbreak of the Civil War, Ely was living in Paterson, New Jersey and employed at the Rogers Locomotive Works. Paterson, New Jersey was, at the time, the home of five manufacturers of locomotives. The largest of these manufacturers was Rogers Locomotive Works, which rolled its first locomotive off the production line in 1837 and became the largest of the locomotive manufacturers.

William Ely returned to Connecticut and joined with the First Connecticut Regiment. He was soon promoted to captain under General Daniel Tyler. He served as an aide for General E.D. Keyes at the Battle of Bull Run. Promoted to Lieutenant Colonel, he served with the Sixth Connecticut Regiment Volunteers. He was in command of the Sixth Connecticut Regiment Volunteers at the capture of Port Royal, South Carolina and was promoted to colonel of the Eighteenth Regiment Connecticut Volunteers. He was eventually promoted to command of the Second Brigade, Second Division, Army of West Virginia. He was captured along with others of the Eighteenth Regiment at Winchester, Virginia and sent to Libby Prison. He, along with others, tunneled out of Libby Prison and returned to the Shenandoah Valley where he was brevetted brigadier-general.

After his return to civilian life, William Ely served as president of the Reade Paper Company. He also served as treasurer of the Falls Company's Cotton Mills.

Augusta Elizabeth (Greene) Ely died July 25, 1900. William Ely died November 13, 1906.

Francis Adams Goddard (1836-1884)   Sect. 75-13

Francis Goddard's tombstone in the Yantic Cemetery flies a Confederate flag.

Francis Goddard was born July 24, 1836 in Connecticut, son of James B. Goddard (1806-1875) of Connecticut and Jane N. Goddard (1816-1884) of Virginia. According to the census, in 1850 they were living in New Rochelle, New York.

When the Civil War began, Francis Adams Goddard enlisted in the Alabama Montgomery Light Artillery Battery, 3rd Infantry Regiment Alabama, Company G. The unit was known as the Montgomery True Blues. He enlisted as a private on April 26, 1861 and was discharged as a corporal.

Francis Goddard died August 17, 1884 in New York and was brought back to Norwich to be buried in the Goddard family plot.

Henry C. Irish (1842-1921)   Sect. 34-11

Henry Clay Irish died in Togus, Maine in 1921. Togus, Maine was the site of the Eastern Branch of the National Home for Disabled Volunteer Soldiers, the first of such homes for soldiers, specifically of the Civil War. Henry moved to the Home in 1896.

In 1858, a resort designed for tourists was built in Togus, Maine by Horace Beals. Beals had earned his fortune as a granite dealer from Rockland, Maine.   The business venture never succeeded and was closed in 1861. In 1866, the U.S. Government bought the property which included a stable, swimming pool, race track and bowling alley. The facility was opened for the soldiers by October of 1866. The facility was comparable to a self-contained small village. The soldiers could work at such places as the bakery, the boot/shoe factory or soap works to name a few. Farming was a big part of the community, as was the blacksmith shop.   The Kennebunc Central Railroad begun in 1890 would take the residents and visitors to and from Togus and Gardiner, a distance of about 8 miles.

Togus: Down in Maine
The First National Veterans Home.
Published by *Images of America.*

Henry Clay Irish was born in New London, Connecticut in 1842, the son of Jedediah Randall Irish (1811-1860) and Nancy F. (Curns) Irish (1813-1875). He married Sara Eliza Keables on August 11, 1868 in Norwich, Connecticut. She was the daughter of Francis and Eliza (Armstrong) Keables.

During the Civil War, Irish enlisted in Company C, Connecticut 1st Cavalry Regiment on November 25, 1861. He was promoted to Full Corporal on February 1, 1864 and mustered out in October 1864.

His unit, the 1st Cavalry Regiment, was stationed in Baltimore, Maryland. "In the winter of 1862-1863 the regiment moved to Baltimore, Md. to be reorganized and was serving there during the Gettysburg Campaign. It moved to Harper's Ferry, W. Va., July 5, 1863, and did duty skirmishing with the southern cavalry in that vicinity until January, 1864. Col. Erastus Blakeslee became the regimental commander. The regiment served in Sheridan's Shenandoah Valley Campaign from August to December. It fought at Cedar Creek, Ream's Station, Five Forks, Yellow Tavern, and Sailor's Creek. It was the 1st CT that escorted Gen. Grant to receive Lee's surrender at Appomattox. The 1st suffered 772 casualties during the war. This was 56% of its strength attesting to its active campaigning."[7]

Henry and Sara had only been married about one year when Sara died in 1869. By 1870, Henry moved back to the Greenville section of Norwich to reside with his mother. In 1870, his occupation was listed as "carpenter."[8] In 1880, he is listed as a "pattern maker."[9]

In 1896, Henry moved to Togus, Maine and there he remained until his passing on November 23, 1921. His brother, still living in Norwich, was in charge of arrangements and had him brought back to Norwich to be interred in the Yantic Cemetery.

Eastern Branch Home, Togus, Maine (no known restrictions on publication as per loc. gov.).

7 www.civil-war-history.com/photo2.html
8 *Norwich Stedman Directory,* 1870.
9 *Norwich Stedman Directory,* 1880.

The Andersonville Nine

At the end of the Civil War, there was a concerted effort by the city of Norwich to retrieve our war dead from the horrific prisoner-of-war camp, Andersonville Prison, located in Georgia. There were sixteen soldiers from Norwich that died in Andersonville, but only nine could be positively identified. These nine soldiers were brought back together. On February 1, 1866, the town turned out for the memorial service held downtown and a procession was made to the Yantic Cemetery.

George W. Smith was the man chosen from Norwich to travel to Georgia to retrieve the bodies of the soldiers. His story is included in this chapter, as well as the life stories of the nine.

Although a couple of these soldiers are buried with their families in family plots as specified in their stories, most are buried in the Soldier's Circle, which is located in Section 67. The section is easily recognized by the flagpole in the middle, next to the cannon, and surrounded by concentric circles of memorial stones from that war, as well as other wars.

George W. Smith (1813-1890)   Sect. 124-7

George Washington Smith was the man responsible for bringing back the war dead from the Andersonville Prison in Andersonville, Georgia in 1866.

Born on November 11, 1813 in East Haddam, Connecticut, George was the son of Asa and Mary Smith. His wife, Adeline A. Palmer Smith, born in 1815, was also born in Connecticut.

George Smith became a cabinet maker. Before coming to Norwich, he served as a cabinet maker apprentice in Hartford, Connecticut, and maintained a cabinet maker's business in Webster, Massachusetts. In Norwich, he worked with George A. Pratt, furniture maker. Smith was at one time the assistant postmaster of Norwich, as well as the assessor.

George Smith's venture to bring back our war dead from Andersonville was funded by the Patriotic Fund Committee. At the outbreak of the Civil War, the Patriotic Fund Committee was established by local citizens, originally for the purpose of starting up units for those volunteers wanting to serve. This committee also equipped the volunteers. By the middle of April, $14,000 had been raised.

They were also concerned with the care of the families of these soldiers. Some members of the list who had pledged funds for this committee were: H.H. Osgood ($100), Gurdon Chapman ($100), and H.H. Starkweather, the postmaster of Norwich ($50).

On October 30, 1865, there was a "Duty to the Fallen" article that ran in the *Norwich Bulletin.* One family member whose soldier had died in Andersonville had been told that one could obtain a permit for the removal of the body. It had already been established that the families of the soldiers who had been killed in the Shenandoah Valley could claim the bodies. The idea was proposed that the town do so for those who had died in Andersonville Prison. By this time, funds had already been provided for two of the soldiers: Joseph Winship and George W. Ward.

By December 1865, it was determined that those from Norwich buried in Andersonville would be brought back home. By the first of the year of 1866, it was decided that George W. Smith would be the 'agent' in charge.

George W. Smith departed on January 3, 1866, and traveled first to Washington, D.C. to obtain the proper permits, and then a rather circuitous route by railway to Lynchburg, Virginia and eventually to Andersonville, Georgia. He arrived in Andersonville on January 11, 1866. The bodies were transported via rail through the Adams Express Co.[10]

The bodies were prepared and burial of eight of the nine took place on February 1, 1866. George W. Ward's funeral was held the next day, February 2, and he was buried in the Oak Street Cemetery. Even though he is not buried in the Yantic Cemetery, his story has been added because he is part of the Andersonville Nine.

George W. Smith died January 25, 1890. Adeline A. Palmer Smith died February 26, 1891.

---

10 Rick Kane, January 7, 2014.

Edward Blumley (ca. 1825-1864)   Sect. 67 (Soldiers' Circle)

Blumley was a private who enlisted on September 26, 1861, and served in the 8th Connecticut Volunteers, Company D. He was captured in an engagement at Petersburg Railroad, Walthall Junction, Virginia on May 7, 1864.

Edward Blumley lived in the Greenville section of Norwich. His wife was Jane Blumley.

Private Edward Blumley died October 6, 1864 in Andersonville Prison at the age of 39.

Henry F. Champlain (1844-1864)   Sect. 67 (Soldiers' Circle)

Henry F. Champlain (sometimes listed as Champlin) was born October 31, 1844 in Westerly, Rhode Island, the son of Clark Champlain (1811-1881) and Mary A. (Rathbun) Champlain (1811-1877).

Henry F. Champlain enlisted in Company F of the 10th Regiment, Connecticut Volunteers on October 1, 1861. Francis Caulkins tells us in her book[11] that Champlain enlisted at Sprague, Connecticut and was captured while on picket duty near St. Augustine, Florida.

Champlain died on August 11, 1864 and was brought back to Norwich with the others from Andersonville Prison.

---

11 *History of Norwich, Connecticut: From its Possession by the Indian, to the Year 1866,* Francis Manwaring Caulkins, published by the author, pp.682, 692.

William Davis (ca. 1824-1864)   Sect. 67 (Soldiers' Circle)

William Davis served in the 1st Connecticut Cavalry. He was captured at Craig's Church, Virginia in May of 1864.

Davis died in Andersonville on August 30, 1864 after being held for three months.

Sylvanus Downer (1820-1864)   Sect. 81-1

Sylvanus Downer is one of the Andersonville Nine that is not buried in the Soldier's Circle, but he and his wife are buried in Section 81.

Sylvanus Downer was born September 10, 1820 in Thetford, Vermont, the son of James Downer and Hannah Downer (1781-1836). His wife was Emma Ann Elizabeth Downer. Emma Downer was born in Bath, Maine on February 10, 1828, the daughter of David Downer and Jane Drummond. Sylvanus and Emma were married in Thetford, Vermont on March 26, 1848.

Children:
* William Henry Downer (1849-1872)
* Frank A. Downer
* Ada Estele Downer (1860-)

"SYLVANUS DOWNER, Eighteenth Regiment C. V. Died in prison at Andersonville, November 5, 1864. He had been chief engineer of the fire department in Norwich, was captured at Winchester, exchanged, rejoined his regiment, and was promoted Color-sergeant. Afterwards wounded in the battle of Piedmont, he was taken prisoner a second time, and carried to the prison-pen at Andersonville, where he died. Age 44."[12]

Emma continued to live in Norwich, and worked as a seamstress. Sylvanus Downer died on November 5, 1864 and was re-interred with his fellow soldiers in the Yantic Cemetery on February 1, 1866. Emma Downer died in Norwich, Connecticut on March 31, 1911.

---

12   *"History of the Eighteenth Regiment Conn. Volunteers in the War for the Union"*, Walker, William Carey, Chaplain, Norwich, Connecticut, published by the Committee, 1885, p. 388.

William G. Hayward (1830-1864)   Sect. 67 (Soldiers' Circle)

William G. Hayward was born in Griswold, Connecticut in 1830. He enlisted and served as a mechanic with the 18th Connecticut Volunteers. He was captured at Winchester, Virginia, exchanged and rejoined his regiment. He was captured again at Newmarket, Virginia on May 15, 1864.

His first wife was Frances Jane Maynard; she died in 1858. They had one daughter, Jane Frances, born circa 1857.

His second wife, Catherine (Donavan) Hayward, was born in Goshen, Connecticut, the daughter of John Donovan and Margaret Corcoran, and raised in the Thompson area of Connecticut. By 1860, William and Catherine were living in the Norwich area. They had one daughter, Catherine, whom they called Minnie. His wife, Catherine, remarried after the Civil War to Henry Worthington Prince.

William Hayward died at Andersonville, Georgia on September 8, 1864 at the age of 34.

Catherine (Donavan) Hayward Prince died in Hyde Park, Massachusetts ca. 1912.

James S. McDavid (1846-1864)

Sect. 5 & Sect. 67 (Soldiers' Circle)

There are two memorial stones for James S. McDavid. One memorial is with his comrades in the Soldiers' Circle, and the other is with his family in Section 5.

James S. McDavid enlisted as a private in Company K, 1st Connecticut Cavalry in January of 1864. He was captured at Ashland Station, Virginia on June 1, 1864.

James S. McDavid (aka J. Stanley McDavid) was born in Connecticut on November 23, 1846, the son of James and Elizabeth McDavid, who were both born in Scotland. James, the father, is listed as a factory laborer. Another son of James and Elizabeth, George H. McDavid (the other name pictured here on the tombstone), was one year younger than James. They were two of seven children of James and Elizabeth.

James S. McDavid died in Andersonville Prison in August 1864 at the age of "17 years & 9 months" according to the stone.

110

Edward F. Tisdale (1845-1864)   Sect. 67 (Soldiers' Circle)

Edward Frank Tisdale was only 15 in November of 1861 when he enlisted in the 9th Connecticut Volunteers. He served in Company H of the 9th Regiment and was discharged the following October because of a disability. He enlisted again in January 1864, this time in the 1st Connecticut Cavalry, Company B. He was captured when his horse was shot out from under him.

Edward Frank Tisdale was born in 1845 in Newburyport, Massachusetts, the son of (Reuben) Rodney Tisdale (1812-1857) and Jane E. Cordeau (-1893).

Tisdale died in Andersonville Prison on September 23, 1864 at the age of 18. The cause of his death was listed as scorbutus, another word for scurvy, caused from a lack of vitamin C.

Edward F. Tisdale was laid to rest with the other soldiers from Andersonville Prison in February 1866.

George W. Ward (ca. 1836-1865)   Oak Street Cemetery

Although George W. Ward is not buried in the Yantic Cemetery, it is appropriate to give him an 'honorable mention' here due to the fact that he was one of the nine brought back to Norwich from Andersonville Prison in February of 1866.

George Washington Ward was born in Connecticut about 1836, the son of Henry Ward and Nancy E. (Huntington) Ward.

George Ward was an organist and a music teacher. He joined the 18th Connecticut Volunteers, and served in Company C. He was taken prisoner at Winchester, Virginia. He was kept there for some time, then transferred to Bell Isle (an island in the James River, Richmond, Virginia), then to Danville, Virginia, and transferred again to Andersonville, Georgia. He died after 21 months of confinement.

Francis Caulkins said of George Ward: "his manly fortitude and genial temperament long sustained him, but continued hunger, confinement, and ill usage at length brought him to the grave... He had fine musical talents, was a steadfast patriot, and had many warm personal friends."[13]

George W. Ward died in February 1865 and is buried in the family plot in the Oak Street Cemetery, Norwich, Connecticut.

---

13 *History of Norwich, Connecticut, from its Possession by the Indians to the Year 1866;* Francis Manwaring Caulkins, published by the author, 1866, p. 691.

Joseph H. Winship (ca. 1841-1864)   Sect. 76-11

Joseph Henry Winship enlisted in the 18th Connecticut Volunteers and served as a clerk. He was left behind after the battle of Winchester, Virginia to take care of the sick and wounded. It was there he was captured on June 16, 1863 and sent to Richmond, Virginia. He was transferred from there to Andersonville Prison.

Joseph Henry Winship was born in Connecticut, the only son of Joseph F. Winship (1804-1885) and Mary H. (Gulliver) Winship (1807-1887). The father, Joseph F. Winship, worked in pottery for many years in Norwich. It is said the death of their only son left the "home of his parents desolate."[14]

Joseph Winship is one of the few soldiers from Andersonville not buried with his comrades in the Soldiers' Circle, but is in the Winship family plot in Section 76.

Joseph H. Winship died in Andersonville on March 5, 1864 (some records, including his stone, show April 5, 1864).

---

14 *History of Norwich, Connecticut: From its Possession by the Indian, to the Year 1866,* Francis Manwaring Caulkins, published by the author, p. 692.

War of 1812

Anson Martin (ca. 1794-1880)   Sect. 7-4

Anson Martin served in the War of 1812 as a private in Captain George Swift's Company of the Connecticut Militia, the 5th Regiment of the Connecticut Militia.

Anson Martin was a wine dealer in civilian life in Norwich. By 1870, he had retired.

Anson Martin and his wife, Harriet F. Martin, were both born in Connecticut. Anson was born circa 1794 and Harriet was born circa 1797.

Children listed to them:
- Sterling Anson Martin (1828-1884); early occupation listed as moulder; born in Pennsylvania, married in 1860 in Indiana to Sarah Angeline Abbot (1832-1908); later occupation was wood carver; served in Union Army during Civil War, 37th Regiment, Indiana Infantry; moved to Dayton, Ohio ca. 1881; died January 12, 1884; buried in National Cemetery, Dayton, Ohio
- Earl S. Martin (ca.1830-1891), born in Pennsylvania
- George E. Martin (ca.1842-1867), born in Connecticut, died in Shanghai, China August 6, 1867 at age 25

Postcard of Shanghai, China.

Postcard of Shanghai, China.

Research of George Martin has not turned up any information as to why he was in Shanghai at that particular time. The above two photographs, even though they were more than likely taken at a much later date, give a fairly good description of what life was like in Shanghai in the 1860's when George Martin was there.

Harriet Martin died April 14, 1871 at the age of 74. Anson Martin died January 25, 1880.

World War II

Wilson Brown, Adm. USN (1882-1957)
Sect. 26-1 (Evergreen Circle)

It is a simple stone, a stone that merely reads "Wilson Brown, Admiral U.S. Navy" and the dates of April 27, 1882 and January 2, 1957. Next to him is his wife Lydia Ballou Brown, the dates of November 5, 1881 and August 27, 1961. The simple inscription gives no indication of his four decades of naval service, including World War I and World War II.

Wilson Brown was born in Pennsylvania on April 27, 1882 and graduated from the Naval Academy in 1902. In 1910, Brown was a lieutenant stationed aboard the *USS Montana.* According to an online article about the *ACR-13 USS Montana/USS Missoula,* this ship was built in Virginia and commissioned in 1908. She was a sister ship of the *USS North Carolina* and both ships had on board the "new wireless radio sets."[15]

Admiral Brown had served in World War I as a staff officer in the Naval Forces in European waters. In 1929, he became the Commanding Officer of the Submarine Base, New London. In 1932, he accepted the command of the *California.* In 1938, he was superintendent of the Naval Academy.

---

15 http://freepages.military.rootsweb.ancestry.com/~cacunithistories/USS_Montana.html

Admiral Wilson Brown was one of the oldest officers to serve in World War II. When World War II broke out, he was Commander of the Scouting Force (re-designated as Patrol Aircraft, Pacific Fleet). He also commanded the *USS Parker*. Just prior to the attack on Pearl Harbor, he "was placed in command of the *Lexington* task force."[16] He was eventually assigned to Task Force 5, and assisted Admiral Halsey's Task Force 8, who was sent to Wake Island. *Lexington* and Task Force 12 (Rear Admiral John H. Newton, commanding) were sent to Midway, and "Vice Admiral Wilson Brown's cruisers of Task Force 5 headed south to conduct landing exercises at Johnston Island... a third of the way between Hawaii and the easternmost of the Marshall [Islands]."[17]

Just after the attack at Pearl Harbor, it was stated that "the immediate task, facing the fleet was to shake off the shock and confusion... Admiral Wilson Brown with [the] *Indianapolis* had added his heavy cruisers to Task Force 12."[18]

Wilson became Rear Admiral in 1942. By then he was almost 60 years old. His next assignment was that of President Franklin Delano Roosevelt's aide and Naval advisor. He retired in 1944, after an illustrious 43 year career in the Navy. He would continue his role as naval advisor until the end of the war.

Admiral Wilson Brown served as *aide-de-camp* to President Franklin Roosevelt. He would eventually serve as aide to two other presidents, President Calvin Coolidge and President Herbert Hoover. A website of online images contains a wonderful photograph of Admiral Brown receiving a medal from President Roosevelt, and another image showing President Roosevelt standing and being supported by Admiral Brown.

Admiral Wilson Brown died in New Haven on January 2, 1957. Lydia (Ballou) Brown died August 27, 1961.

---

16   http://pwencycl.kgbudge.com/Pacific War Online Encyclopedia: Brown, Wilson, Jr.
17   *"And I Was There": Pearl Harbor and Midway - Breaking the Secrets* by Rear Admiral Edwin T. Layton, U.S.N. (Ret.), with Captain Roger Pineau, U.S.N.R. (Ret.), and John Costello, William Morrow and Company, Inc., New York, p. 223.
18   Ibid, p. 325.

VIII.

Missionary Stories

James Howie (c. 1826-1877)   Sect. 113-23

There is only a single marker in this plot with the family name, but apparently most of the family, including James Howie, his wife Susan, daughters Nellie and Maggie, and son-in-law Charles Tracy, are buried in this plot.

James Howie was born in Scotland circa 1826. His occupation is listed as cork cutter. His wife Susan Howie was born in Connecticut circa 1839. Their daughter Margaret (Maggie) was born in New York circa 1851. She married Charles Tracy on July 3, 1872. Charles Tracy had an interesting lineage. Charles was born on March 17, 1849 in Pasumalai, India, the son of the missionary Reverend William Tracy and his wife Emily Francis (Travelli) Tracy (1811-1879). Reverend Tracy died on the mission field in Tirupuvanam, India in 1877.

Nellie, daughter of James and Susan Howie, was born in Connecticut circa 1867. Nellie Howie died January 4, 1948 at the age of 80.

James Howie died December 7, 1877 at the age of 51. After her husband died, Susan worked at a variety store on Franklin Street, Norwich. She outlived her husband by thirty-five years and died September 12, 1912 at the age of 74.

Edward H. Smith (1873-1968)   Sect. 98-15

Edward Huntington Smith and his wife Grace were missionaries to China. Edward H. Smith was a missionary for almost 50 years, including operating an orphanage, and was involved with various missionary efforts from 1901 to 1950. His wife Grace taught kindergarten in the United States as well as in China. Grace died on the mission field and is buried in China.

Children:
- Helen Huntington Smith, born in Yung-t'ai, China on December 19, 1902, died circa 1971
- Edward Huntington Smith, Jr., born (probably in China) circa 1905
- Eunice Elizabeth Smith Bishop, born in Foochow, China, May 24, 1906
- Margaret Thomas Smith, born in Foochow, China, October 2, 1912

Edward H. Smith was born July 1, 1873 in Franklin, Connecticut, the son of Owen S. Smith and Hattie E. Huntington. Grace (Thomas) Smith, wife of Edward, was born in Pine Brook, New Jersey in 1874, the daughter of Reverend James S. Thomas and Eunice D. (Drake) Thomas. They were married on October 2, 1901 by her father, who at the time was a pastor in Holbrook, Massachusetts.

Because of the Boxer Rebellion at the turn of the 20th century, they had to return to the United States. By June of 1915, they had returned to Yung-t'ai, China as missionaries with the ABCFM (American Board of Commissioners for Foreign Missions).

Grace Thomas Smith is buried in China. According to the "Report of the Death of an American Citizen, American Foreign Service" on ancestry.com, Grace died July 21, 1939 in the Willis F. Pierce Hospital, Foochow, China and is "Interred in the American Cemetery, Foochow, China, near the south end, on the west side of main walk."

Certificate of Registration of American Citizen (in China).

Edward H. Smith returned from the foreign field in 1950. He died in Massachusetts on November 6, 1968 at the age of 95, and was returned to Norwich to be buried in the Smith family plot.

The online archive of the University of Southern California (USC Digital Library) has a number of photographs of the Edward H. Smith family and of their work in Foochow (Fuzhou), China.

IX.

Policemen

John A. Bowen, Police Chief (1843-1910)   Sect. 121-3

John A. Bowen was born in Voluntown, Connecticut on May 25, 1843. At the age of 7, he moved with his family to Westerly, Rhode Island.[1] At the outbreak of the Civil War, he enlisted at Mystic, Connecticut and served about 3 years attaining the rank of sergeant. He was a prisoner at Libby prison and Belle Isle prison, both located in the Richmond, Virginia area.

At the end of the Civil War in 1865, he married Eleanor Arnold of Westerly, Rhode Island (born in 1843). They had one son, Philip E. Bowen (1866-1958) who moved to Los Angeles, California.

In 1869, John A. Bowen began his career as a policeman. He was promoted to sergeant in 1880, made first sergeant in 1883, captain of the night watch in 1886, and made Chief of Police in 1889. Bowen became "the first *paid* Police Chief of Norwich, Connecticut."[2]

---

1 *Norwich Evening Record - Souvenir Edition,* Cleworth and Pullen, published 1894, reprinted 1993, Franklin Impressions, page 19.
2 *"Biographical Review, Vol. XXVI - Containing Life Sketches of Leading Citizens of New London County Connecticut"*, Boston, Biography Review Publishing Co., 1898; pp. 104-107.

John A. Bowen died in Norwich on November 1, 1910. Eleanor Bowen died in East Lyme, Connecticut on October 14, 1931.

Picture from the *Norwich Evening Record - souvenir edition,*
reprinted 1993 by Franklin Impressions.

Charles S. Ebberts (1849-1926)   Sect. 113

Charles Ebberts was with the police department in Norwich from 1878 until just about the time of his death in 1926.

Charles Sylvester Ebberts was born on December 3, 1849 in Maryland. In 1870, he was living in Washington, D.C. In 1871, he married Eliza Jane Matthews, who was born in Ireland in 1846, the daughter of John and Mary Matthews. Eliza died in 1895.

Children:
- Mary Emma Ebberts (1872-), worked as wafer slicer in cork shop in 1900
- Henrietta Elizabeth Ebberts (1876-)
- Ida Sylvester Ebberts (1882-1947)
- Isabell Ann Ebberts (1884-), listed as nurse girl in 1900

Charles' second wife, Catherine A. (Borden) Ebberts, sometimes listed as 'Kathleen,' was born in Rhode Island in September 1868. They were married in 1896. Her parents were both from Massachusetts.

Ebberts took part in the parade at the 250th anniversary celebration of the founding of Norwich, which took place in July of 1909. In a pamphlet written for the occasion, there is a description of the parade: "Promptness and efficiency marked the management and formation of the various divisions... There had been no hitch in getting the various divisions assembled... In the lead were Sergeant Twomey and Policemen Ebberts and Doty, mounted."[3]

Catherine Ebberts died in 1921. Charles S. Ebberts died July 17, 1926 at the age of 75.

---

3 *"The celebration of the two hundred and fiftieth anniversary of the settlement of the town of Norwich, Connecticut, and of the incorporation of the city, the one hundred and twenty-fifth, July 4, 5, 6, 1909"*, program printed for the celebration.

X.

Reverends, Preachers and Pastors

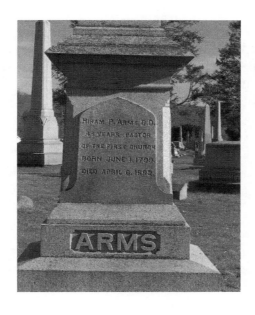

Reverend Hiram P. Arms, D.D. (1799-1882)   Section 86-10

Hiram Phelps Arms was the son of William Arms IV (1769-1813) and Mercy Snow (1767-1817), and a grandson of William Arms III (1724-1794) and Elizabeth Belding (1723-1804) of Deerfield, Massachusetts. Hiram was born in Windsor, Connecticut on June 1, 1799.

Reverend Arms graduated from Yale and was ordained at Hebron, Connecticut on June 30, 1830, although he had preached for several years before that. After his ordination, he taught at private schools in New Haven as well as the Kingston Academy, New York, pictured here.

Postcard of the Kingston Academy, New York.

He preached at Sing Sing, New York and at Longmeadow, Massachusetts, and served as pastor in Wolcottville, Connecticut before settling in Norwich. He was installed as pastor of the First Congregational Church of Norwich in 1836, and remained their active pastor for 37 years, retiring at the age of 74. He continued as *pastor emeritus* for another 8 years, for a total service of 45 years.

Reverend Arms married twice. He married his first wife, Lucy Ann Wadhams of New Haven on September 12, 1824. She died July 3, 1837, leaving 4 of her 5 children. He married his second wife, Sarah 'Abby' Jane Baker (1803-1878) of New York, on September 12, 1838.

Children of Hiram and Lucy Arms:
- Catherine Lewis Arms (1825-1826)
- Catherine Bruyn Arms (1828-1895)
- William F. Arms (1831-1905), served as missionary to Armenians in Turkey
- George H. Arms (1833-1878), Civil War engineer/bridge builder, Confederate Army
- Francis T. Arms (1835-1889), Civil War, Union Army
- Lucy A. Arms (1837-1865)

Children of Hiram and Sarah Jane (Baker) Arms:
- Sarah J. Arms (1839-1898), married Reverend William B. Clarke
- Charles Jessop Arms (1841-1901), Colonel in Union Army
- Theodore Winthrop Arms (1844-), Civil War, Union Army

Sarah 'Abby' Jane Arms died August 10, 1878. Reverend Hiram Arms died April 6, 1882.

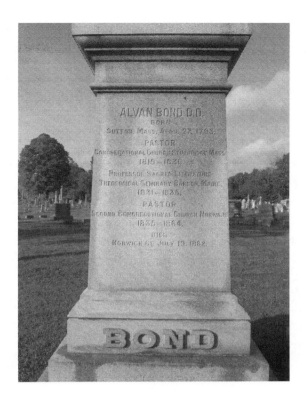

Reverend Alvan Bond, D.D. (1793-1882)   Sect. 83-3

Alvan Bond's gravestone has much of his life's history posted on it. It states that Alvan Bond was born in Sutton, Massachusetts on April 27, 1793. It also lists the churches of which he was the pastor including the Congregational Church in Sturbridge, Massachusetts (4 years) and the Second Congregational Church in Norwich (29 years). It also reads that he was professor of sacred literature at the Theological Seminary in Maine (4 years), and we find that he died in July of 1882.

Reverend Bond graduated from Brown University with a degree as Doctor of Divinity.[1] From the church history of the church in Sturbridge, Massachusetts, we find this reference to Reverend Bond who had just recently graduated, "a [yearly] salary of $600 was voted to him."[2]

Reverend Bond was married to Sarah Richardson on April 25, 1821. Sarah Richardson was born in Medway, Massachusetts on September 27, 1796, the daughter of Ezra Richardson and Jemima Lovell (1767-1826). Sarah died August 12, 1834. In May 1836, Bond married Mehitabel A. Bull, born circa 1801. She

---

1 *History of Norwich, Connecticut: from its possession by the Indians to the year 1866*, p. 555.
2 *The Historical Sketch of the First Congregational Church, Sturbridge, Mass,* pp. 29-30.

died October 4, 1844. In September 1850, Bond married Sibby Ann W. Davis (born ca. 1809) of Concord, Massachusetts; she died June 10, 1876.

Children of Sarah (Richardson) Bond and Alvan Bond:
- Sarah Elizabeth Bond (1822-1846)
- Abigail (Abby) L. Bond (1823-)
- William Cyrus Bond (1825-1826)
- Alvan Cyrus Bond (1826-1847)
- William Cyrus Bond (1828-)
- Francis (Frank) Stuart Bond (1830-1912), Lieutenant and Aide-de-Camp in Civil War, died at Jekyll Island, Georgia
- Henry Richardson Bond (1832-1909)
- Louisa Waters Bond (1834-1927)

Children of Mehitabel (Bull) Bond and Alvan Bond:
- Anna Bond (1841-1841)
- Mary Bond (1843-1844)

But that does not tell the whole story. Dr. Alvan Bond, among others, was instrumental in bringing eleven Native American boys of the Chickasaw/Choctaw tribe from Oklahoma to be educated at the Plainfield Academy in Plainfield, Connecticut (pictured here).

In the 1840's, Peter P. Pitchlynn, Choctaw chief also known as Hat-choo-tuck-nee (the snapping turtle), had been assigned as education 'agent' for the Chickasaw and Choctaw nations for their youth. He would decide where/when the boys would be sent to school. Many of the young men were brought out east to attend schools; some to Kentucky, some to Delaware College, Newark, Delaware, and some to the Plainfield Academy in Connecticut. In the summer of 1848, Pitchlynn, along with eleven boys from the Choctaw tribe, arrived at the Plainfield Academy.[3] And so it was on August 22, 1848, these boys with such names as Samuel Colbert, Tecumseh Gaines and Jefferson Greenwood began their studies. Eventually they would number nineteen. They lived with the families of Dr. William Cogswell, Elisha Lord Fuller, Henry Phillips, and later on Elkanah C. Eaton, Jr. In 1849, Dr. Bond reported to their guardian, Peter Pitchlynn, that "the young men had learned to read quite well, 'spell with a good degree of accuracy', and 'write a fair hand.' "[4] This arrangement lasted from 1848 to 1852. The most difficult thing the boys had to deal with was the climate. Two boys died while

---

3 *"Chronicles of Oklahoma, Volume XV, Number 2, June 1937"*, article titled *Education Among the Chickasaw Indians*, by Carolyn Thomas Foreman.
4 Ibid., p. 158.

living in Plainfield and are buried in the Plainfield cemetery. "Communication between the Indians and Plainfield was long maintained by letters, chiefly from Samuel Colbert (one of the first boys in the program) to the Cogswell family, until after the war in 1861."[5]

Reverend Bond's church was located on Church Street in Norwich, Connecticut. It was also said of Reverend Bond that it was through his influence and encouragement to one of his parishioners, Joseph Otis (found near the end of the book), that the Otis Library was established in Norwich.

Reverend Alvan Bond died July 19, 1882.

---

5 Ibid., p. 165, as quoted from *The Chautauquan,* March 1894, pp. 707-711.

Reverend William B. Clarke (1829-1905)   Sect. 98-10

Reverend William Barker Clarke was born December 27, 1829 in Gibara, Cuba, the youngest of ten children born to George Asahel Clarke (1781-1830) and Mary Ann Jessup (1794-1856).

His father George A. Clarke had established a business with his brother in Gibara, Cuba and in 1822 moved the family there. Just two years later, in 1824, they would lose five of their children to a fever which swept the island. After George died in 1830, Mary moved with the five remaining children back to the states. Only two (or possibly three) children survived to adulthood.

Clarke graduated from Yale College in 1849 and Yale Theological Seminary in 1852. He pastored in West Cornwall, Connecticut for several years. He was Professor of Sacred Theology for several years and pastored in Litchfield, Connecticut from 1866 until 1871. He preached in Griswold, Connecticut and in 1884 moved to Norwichtown, Connecticut.

William Clarke married Sarah Jane Arms on April 18, 1866. Sarah Arms was the daughter of Reverend Hiram Arms, pastor of the Norwichtown Congregational Church for many years, and his wife Sarah Jane (Baker) Arms.

Children:
- Helen McGregor Clarke (1867-)
- Jane Baker Clarke (1868-)
- Francisco Arms Clarke (1879-1881)

Sarah Jane Clarke died in Durham, Connecticut on November 9, 1898. Reverend William B. Clarke died in Durham on September 18, 1905.

Reverend Malcolm M.G. Dana, D.D. (1838-1897)   Sect. 63

Reverend Malcolm McGregor Dana was pastor of the Second Congregational Church, Norwich for 10 years (1864-1874). He was also pastor of the Park Congregational Church from 1874 until 1878.

Malcolm McGregor Dana was born in Brooklyn, New York in 1838, the son of Alex Hop Dana, a lawyer who distinguished himself in Brooklyn, and his wife Augusta Dana. He graduated from Amherst College in 1859 and from the Union Theological Seminary in New York in 1863. His wife, Susan Clark Dana, was born circa 1838 in Massachusetts.

Dana was ordained the pastor of the Second Congregational Church in 1864. He served the church until 1874, when "Dr. Dana resigned, and with one hundred and five of his old members, formed the Park Congregational Church [Norwich, Connecticut]."[6] He would be pastor of that church until 1878.

In 1878, with his wife Susan being ill, he headed west and became the pastor of the Plymouth Congregational Church, St. Paul, Minnesota.

Children:
- Lucius C. Dana, born in Connecticut (1867-1894)
- Malcolm M. Dana, Jr., born in Connecticut circa 1870
- Frank V.N. Dana, born in Connecticut circa 1874
- Freddie (1875-1877)
- Mary H. Dana, born in Minnesota circa 1878

Susan Clark Dana died November 19, 1886 in St. Paul, Minnesota and was brought back to Norwich to be buried. Reverend Malcolm Dana died July 25, 1897 in Brooklyn, New York and was also brought back to Norwich.

---

6 *New London County, Connecticut: A Modern History;* editor-in-chief Benjamin Tinkham Marshall, 1872, New York, Lewis Historical Publishing Company, 1922.

Reverend Anson Gleason (1797-1885)   Sect. 10-1

Reverend Anson Gleason was a missionary to the Choctaw Indians for a number of years. After his return to Connecticut in 1830, he worked with the Mohegan Indians for sixteen years. He was ordained as a Congregational minister in 1835.

Anson Gleason was born in Manchester, Connecticut on May 2, 1797. His wife, Bethiah W. Tracy, was born in Franklin, Connecticut on January 20, 1803. Bethiah Tracy and Anson Gleason were married on October 26, 1826. Eight children are listed to them.

In 1855, the Gleasons moved to Westfield, New York and served on the church staff. 'Father Gleason' as he came to be known was described as "kindly and forceful with a grand personality and persuasive voice." The article goes on to say, "... that soul-stirring hymn which was his favorite, 'Come, Thou Fount of Every Blessing,' which he sang with the greatest zest..."[7]

From 1858 to 1861, he worked on the Six Nations Cattaraugus Reservation in western New York, and thereafter did city mission work in Rochester, Utica and Brooklyn, New York. In Brooklyn at the end of the Civil War, he was employed part time at the Mission Sabbath School of the Central Congregational Church.

Father Gleason died in Brooklyn, New York on February 24, 1885 and was brought back to Norwich to be buried in the Yantic Cemetery.

---

7 *The Centennial History, First Presbyterian Church, Westfield,* Chautauqua Co., N.Y.

Included in his obituary is this description of the funeral procession: "As the body was taken into the Yantic Cemetery in this city, yesterday afternoon, a little band of the head men and women of the Mohegans followed with bared heads in the funeral train. They had not been invited to attend the ceremonies, but were drawn by feelings of love and reverence to pay the last tribute of their respect to one whose name was a memory bequeathed to them by elders of the tribe who are now dead. As soon as they appeared in the yard they were voluntarily conceded the first place in participating in the rites. Six of them acted as pallbearers, and after they had borne the casket to the side of the grave they [ar]ranged themselves in the bright sunlight on each side of it, and sang hymns, marked by the peculiar Indian death song intonation. Tears ran down their cheeks."[8]

Reverend Anson Gleason was laid to rest on February 28, 1885. Bethiah Gleason died in Brooklyn, New York on October 13, 1886 and is buried next to her husband.

---

8 http://www.findagrave.com/cgi-
bin/fg.cgipage=gr&GSln=Gleason&GSiman=1&GScid=103847&GRid=32608407&

Reverend Martin Ham Rising (1821-1880)   Section 19-7

As far as I know, Martin Ham Rising is the only person in the Yantic Cemetery that I can claim as family. I stumbled upon this stone of a Rising, my mother's maiden name, and found him in my collective genealogy.

Martin Ham Rising was born in Massachusetts on February 15, 1821. At some point, his family moved to Suffield, Connecticut. Martin Rising originally pursued medicine, but changed his life's work to that of the ministry. At the age of 24, Reverend Martin H. Rising became the pastor of the First Baptist Church of Norwich, Connecticut, where he was the pastor from 1846 to 1849. In 1846, Rising had come to the Norwich area for a vacation, but "the interest of the [First Baptist] church was so great, he was compelled to remain, or to use his own words, he 'did not dare to go back.' " He had served the pulpit for a few months, but he was called as their pastor March 3, 1846, and "was ordained the following day."[9] He resigned in 1849 due to ill health. Under his pastorate, the church

---

9 *Eighty-Four Years of Baptist Ministry,* First Baptist Church, Norwich, Connecticut, *p. 31.*

experienced quite a revival, and acquired land for the purpose of a new church building.

Martin Rising's spouse was Mary A. Breed. She was born in Norwich in 1824. Her father was Benjamin F. Breed, a blacksmith in Norwich, Connecticut, and her mother was Mary A. Breed. Martin and Mary must have met through her father, Benjamin, who had become a deacon of the church about the same time that Reverend Rising became their pastor. Martin and Mary were married in the Baptist Church of Jewett City, Connecticut.

Reverend Rising would go on to have two other short stints as pastor, but "his incessant work brought on weaknesses that prostrated him for more than twenty years."[10]

Martin Ham Rising died August 30, 1880. Mary died in Perth Amboy, New Jersey on January 12, 1901. Martin and Mary are buried in the Breed family plot.

---

10 Ibid., p. 35.

Reverend John Sterry (1766-1823)   **Sect. 131**

John Sterry was the first pastor of the First Baptist Church, Norwich. He and his brother ran a bookbinding and printing business in Norwich, but people in the fledgling Baptist group recognized his ability to preach, and so it was that in 1800 he was ordained as pastor of the First Baptist Church of Norwich, a position he held for 23 years.

John Sterry was born in Preston, Connecticut (some records say Providence, Rhode Island) on September 24, 1766, son of Captain Roger Sterry. His wife, Rebecca (Bromley) Sterry from Preston, was born in 1776. They were married on October 4, 1792, by Pastor Lemuel Tyler.

Children:
- John Holmes Sterry (1793-1870)
- Margery Davidson Sterry (1796-1836)
- Rebecca Bromley Sterry (1800-1870)
- George Washington Sterry (1807-1823)

- Caroline Sterry (1809-1831)
- Edward Augustus Sterry (1811-1887), married Catherine Whittlesey
- Maria Louisa Sterry (1817-1880)
- William Palmer Sterry (1819-1886)
- Francis Asher Sterry (1821-1902)

Reverend John Sterry died November 7, 1823. Rebecca Sterry died September 10, 1833.

XI.

Scientists

Thomas Sterry Hunt, LL.D. (1826-1892)   Section 81-12

Thomas Sterry Hunt was a scientist, geologist, chemist and mineralogist. Hunt was born in Norwich on September 5, 1826, the son of Peleg Hunt (1800-1838) and Jane Elizabeth (Sterry) Hunt (1803-1866). His father died when he was just 12 years old and he had to begin to work for a living at the age of 13.

Hunt's first "formal introduction to the world of science" was in 1845 at the Sixth Annual Meeting of the Association of American Geologists and Naturalists, held in New Haven, Connecticut.[1] He befriended Benjamin Silliman, Jr., professor of chemistry, who was able to get Hunt into the Scientific School of Yale University. During the two year span of 1845 to 1847, he contributed numerous articles to *Silliman's Journal*.

---

1 *National Academy Biographical Memoirs* - Vol. XV, p. 208.

The Geological Survey of Canada had been established in 1842, and was looking for a chemist and mineralogist. Thomas Sterry Hunt came highly recommended from Mr. Silliman. In 1847 he began this position, and for the next 25 years he would work and live in Canada.

From 1856 to 1862, he gave a course of lectures in the spring at Laval University in Quebec. He also lectured at the McGill University in Montreal.

In 1857, he developed the ink for the money that came to be known as "greenbacks." Hunt "...suggested the use of sesquioxide of chromium as the basis of a green ink for printing bank notes, it being a substance which could not be removed by either an acid or an alkali without destroying the paper and which also could not be satisfactorily photographed. This invention was patented and being subsequently adopted in the United States for the printing of 'greenbacks' became very valuable, but Hunt himself never reaped any substantial reward from his discovery."[2]

In 1872, he accepted the Professorship of Geology at Massachusetts Institute of Technology, but teaching did not particularly suit him.

In 1875, he went back to doing field work. From 1875 to 1878, he did extensive field work in southeastern Pennsylvania under J.P. Lesley with the Second Geological Survey of Pennsylvania. In 1878, the first of two volumes he was expected to write as a result of this exploration was published: "Special Report of the Trap Dykes and Azoic Rocks of Southeastern Pennsylvania."

He had a wide knowledge of the natural and physical sciences. He was said to have "an outstanding personality." He was also said to have a "peculiar charm of manner... and was a brilliant conversationalist."[3]

He did not marry until later in life. In 1878, he married Anna Rebecca Gale (1853-), the daughter of Mr. Justice Gale of Montreal.

He had served as president of several organizations:
- American Association for the Advancement of Science (1870)
- American Institute of Mining Engineers (1876)
- American Chemical Society (1879 and again in 1888)
- Royal Society of Canada (1884)

His last two years he spent either at the St. Luke's Hospital, New York or at the Park Avenue Hotel in New York. He continued to write up to the very end of his life. He died in New York City on February 12, 1892.

---

2 *National Academy Biographical Memoirs* - Vol. XV, p. 217.
3 Ibid.

David Ames Wells (1827-1898)   Sect. 88-9, 10

David Ames Wells was a political economist, engineer, scientist and author. He was born in Springfield, Massachusetts on June 17, 1827. In 1847, he graduated from Williams College which is located in Williamsburg, Massachusetts. Immediately after graduation, he began working for the *Springfield Republican,* Springfield, Massachusetts.

In 1849, he enrolled in the Lawrence Scientific School of Harvard, and graduated from there in 1852. After graduation, he was hired on as an assistant professor.

From 1857 to 1863, he "was engaged in the preparation of a series of scientific school books... an elementary treatise on chemistry – was adopted as a text-book at West Point..."[4]

During the Civil War, he wrote and published a pamphlet entitled "Our Burden and Our Strength" demonstrating the financial strength of the federal government. It enjoyed a wide circulation, even in Europe.

---

4 "The Popular Science Monthly," *Sketch of David Ames Wells,* Vol. XXXII, p. 833.

Wells was appointed Special Commissioner of the U.S. Internal Revenue from 1866 to 1870, and was hired to find the "best methods of dealing... with the enormous debt and burden of taxation..."[5]

In 1872, after his retirement from federal work, he was appointed by the governor of New York to investigate that state's revenue, as he had done with the federal government. He held that position until 1873.

He was quite involved with the railroad, particularly with the Alabama & Chattanooga and the New York & Erie Railroads. He also served on the railroad's national board of arbitration.

The following are just some of the organizations on which Wells served: president of the New London Historical Society, national board of visitors at West Point, president of the Social Science Association and president of the American Free Trade League.

Wells' writings and publications were many. Amongst them: "Why We Trade and How We Trade" and "Robinson Crusoe's Money." He also wrote "A Study of Mexico," "The Dollar of the Fathers vs. the Dollar of the Sons" and "A Primer of Wages."

David Wells was married twice. His first wife, Mary Sandford (Dwight) Wells, the daughter of James and Elizabeth Dwight, was born in Springfield, Massachusetts on October 13, 1826. She and David were married on May 9, 1860. Mary died on January 27, 1877. They had one son, David Dwight Wells (1868-1900).

In 1879, he married his second wife, Ellen Augusta Dwight, sister of his first wife, Mary. Ellen was born in Springfield, Massachusetts on July 23, 1829.

David Ames Wells died on November 5, 1898. Ellen Augusta Wells died December 12, 1898, just five weeks after her husband.

---

5 Ibid.

XII.

Teachers and Educators

Matilda Butts (1856-1934)   Sect. 89-7

The Butts family roots go deep into the heart and the soil of New England and in Connecticut. Matilda Butts' great-great-grandfather, Captain Sherebiah Butts (1732-1807) of the Canterbury, Connecticut area, was a patriot and a Revolutionary War soldier. He and his seven sons helped to build the Westminster Congregational Church (pictured here) in Westminster, Connecticut, located on Route 14 in the area of Scotland and Canterbury. Most of Sherebiah Butts' family is buried in the church yard next to the Westminster Congregational Church.

Westminster Congregational Church, Route 14, Canterbury, Connecticut.

Matilda Butts was born in Norwich on January 18, 1856, the daughter of Henry L. Butts and Sarah Ann (Richards) Butts. Her father Henry established a file manufacturing company, the Chelsea File Works, in Norwich. Brother Charles worked in the family business as well.

159

 In 1902, Matilda Butts opened a school for girls on the road that is now known as Washington Street Extension in the house pictured here. The *Norwich Bulletin* published an ad on August 31, 1901 about the opening of the school. The ad reads, "MISS BUTTS'S SCHOOL FOR GIRLS at 'Lowthorpe' will open on Thursday, September 26. Mademoiselle Rivet, a native of Paris, will have charge of the French department, and Miss Haviland, who brings a diploma from Frau Doctor Hempel's Seminar, Berlin, will have charge of the German. Special classes in both languages will be formed for beginners and for advanced pupils. Miss Butts is prepared to receive a limited number of young ladies into her family, and also day pupils of all grades."

The school was at this location for two years before moving to a larger location on Beech Drive in 1904, the magnificent house originally built for Reverend Leonard Bacon. Ms. Butts operated the school until about 1914.

Matilda Butts was a part of the Norwich Red Cross chapter which had opened in 1907 and "took part in the relief work at the time of the San Francisco disaster."[1]

After her retirement from the school, Matilda lived with her sister Adelaide in a house on Washington Street until her death in 1934.

Postcard of Miss Butts' School on Beech Dr, Norwich, CT.

Matilda Butts died September 21, 1934. Adelaide Butts died January 12, 1941.

---

1 *The New London County, Connecticut: A Modern History*, Chapter XXII.

Daniel Coit Gilman (1831-1908)   Sect. 21-8

Daniel Coit Gilman was the founder and first president of the Johns Hopkins University. Born in Norwich, Connecticut on July 6, 1831, he was the son of William Gilman and Eliza (Coit) Gilman. His roots ran deep in Connecticut soil. He was the great-grandson of Ephraim Bill and Lydia (Huntington) Bill, early settlers of Norwich. He spent his early days in Norwich but his family moved to New York when he was of high school age. He entered Yale as a member of the class of 1852. One of his classmates, and a man with whom he would remain lifelong friends, was Andrew White. Andrew White would eventually become the first president of Cornell University.

Daniel Coit Gilman was most interested in the European style of education. In 1853, Gilman and White traveled to Europe, including France, England and Germany "digesting stores of knowledge regarding European education."[2]

He returned to New Haven and Yale and became chief administrator of the Sheffield Scientific School (pictured here). While there, he became acquainted with James Dwight Dana, and eventually wrote his biography. He also became professor of physical geography at Yale.

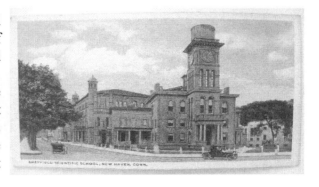

In December of 1861, he married Mary Ketcham (1838-1869) of New York, daughter of Tredwell Ketcham and Mary VanWinker. Mary died in 1869. He

2 Gale Encyclopedia of Biography: Daniel Coit Gilman: http://www.answers.com/topic/daniel-coit-gilman

married his second wife, Elisabeth Dwight Woolsey (1838-1910) in 1877. Elisabeth was the daughter of John M. Woolsey of Cleveland, Ohio and the niece of the president of Yale University, Theodore Dwight Woolsey.

He had two daughters, Alice (who married Everett Wheeler) and Elisabeth Gilman. Elisabeth Gilman, social activist, ran for mayor of Baltimore, Maryland. She was also a candidate for governor, and senator of Maryland on the Socialist Party of America ticket.

In 1872, Daniel Gilman took a position at the University of California, but was there only a brief time.

The wealthy financier Johns Hopkins of Baltimore, Maryland had bequeathed $3.5 million for the founding of a higher education facility. Hopkins had hand-picked twelve trustees several years before his death, and upon his death in 1874 they sought the advice of three well known university presidents: Harvard University president Charles Eliot, James B. Angell of Michigan, and Cornell University president Andrew White. They all agreed that Daniel Coit Gilman

should be president. And so it was that he established and became the first president of Johns Hopkins University in 1875. That very summer he traveled to Europe and began a search of faculty.

Early postcard of Johns Hopkins University.

Johns Hopkins University (public domain).

Daniel Coit Gilman was also chosen as the first president of the Carnegie Institute (1901-1904). Instead of starting a college or university in the city of Washington, D.C., which Carnegie felt might weaken the already existing universities, he decided instead to develop an independent research organization. In Carnegie's words: "It is proposed to found in the city of Washington, an institution which...

162

shall in the broadest and most liberal manner encourage investigation, research, and discovery [and] show the application of knowledge to the improvement of mankind..." — Andrew Carnegie, January 28, 1902.[3]

Gilman also served as president of the American Bible Society from 1903 to 1908. He was elected unanimously and we find this quote regarding that election: "The long vacancy in the office of President has at last been adequately filled in the election of Daniel Coit Gilman, LL.D., one of the Vice-Presidents of the Society, a resident of Baltimore, MD where he has long been a Manager of the Maryland Bible Society."[4]

The Bolton Hill Historic District in Maryland posted a plaque in tribute to him: "Daniel Coit Gilman, 1831-1908: First President of Johns Hopkins University. First director of Johns Hopkins Hospital. A pathfinder in American graduate and professional education."

Daniel Coit Gilman died October 13, 1908 in Maryland and was brought back to Connecticut to be buried. Elizabeth Gilman died in Norwich on January 14, 1910.

---

3 *"The Carnegie Institution of Washington, D.C. Founded by Andrew Carnegie 1902"*, press of the New Era Printing Co., 1902, p. 10.
4 "American Bible History: The Amazing Story of the Quest to Make the Bible Available to Christians in America."

XIII.

Tragedies

Alexander G. Cutler (1835-1880)   Section 1-18

The stone reads in part, "Alexander G. Cutler Lost on the steamer Narragansett June 11, 1880 Aged 45 years."

Born in 1835 in Connecticut, Alexander Cutler was a well respected architect in Norwich for a number of years until his tragic death in 1880. He and his daughter, Euretta G. Cutler, aged "9 years & 9 months" died in the *SS Narragansett* collision with the *SS Stonington* in Long Island Sound on June 11, 1880. There were about 50 casualties, including one crewman, who died in that accident.

At the time of his death, Cutler was working on a project with the Groton Monument. He had been awarded the contract to do the work on the crown of the monument in preparation for the 1881 centennial celebration of the Battle of Groton Heights, Groton, Connecticut. The reason for his visit to New York was for gathering information on costs, materials, etc. He and his daughter died on their return home from New York.

167

The gravestone reads:

Alexander G. Cutler
Lost on the steamer
Narragansett
June 11, 1880
Aged 45 years

Euretta Gordon Cutler
Lost on the steamer
Narragansett
June 11, 1880
Aged 9 years & 9 months

Ella Gordon Cutler
Died April 28, 1869
Aged 8 months

Cutler's wife, Mary J. Cutler was born Mary Jane Leffingwell in Bozrah on September 22, 1838. After the death of her husband and daughter in 1880, she eventually married again. The second marriage was to Jacob Flint Starkweather in January 1909. She died September 11 that same year. She is buried in the West Plains Cemetery in Norwich, Connecticut. Although her children are not buried in West Plains, their names, Euretta and Ella, are listed on the memorial marker.

Mae Caroline Robidoux (1913- 1963)   Sect. 103-8

Caroline Robidoux, as she was known, was one of the six victims to die in the Spaulding Dam disaster on March 6, 1963. Caroline worked at the Turner Stanton Mill located on Broad Street, Norwich. The mill was destroyed by the flood waters when the Spaulding Dam broke.

Mae Caroline Robidoux was the wife of Albert Robidoux. Albert (1908-1998) was born in Canada to Joseph and Jeanne Robidoux. Albert is buried in the Maplewood Cemetery.

Mae Robidoux was laid to rest on March 9, 1963.

Wreck of the Steamship *City of New London,*
November 22, 1871

On November 22, 1871, four men from Norwich perished when the steamer *City of New London* caught on fire in early evening on the Thames River.

The following information was also gleaned from the *New York Times* article, dated November 23, 1871. The steamer was of the Norwich and New York Line, and was commanded by Captain William R. Brown. The flames were first noticed coming from the ventilators. The boat was anchored and the fire was seemingly extinguished. The anchor was hoisted and they proceeded on their trip. In the area abreast of the Poquetannock Cove, fire was once again discovered, this time in some bales of cotton that were stored on deck. The pumps were started and the Captain and crew had water streaming on the fire, but the blaze spread rapidly and soon "enveloped all the forward part of the boat." The life preservers were rendered inaccessible. The passengers and crew threw themselves into the water, clinging to whatever debris or items were found or thrown into the water. The capable swimmers were able to reach the shore with not too much difficulty. Some were picked up by other boats.

What follows are the stories of the four men from Norwich who died on the *City of New London* that fateful day: Harrison R. Aldrich, Matthias (Matthew) Baker, William T. Norton and Caleb B. Rogers.

Harrison R. Aldrich (1828-1871)   Sect. 57-2

Harrison Randolph Aldrich was born in Connecticut in 1828. His wife, sometimes listed as M.J. Aldrich, was Mary Jane (Rogers) Aldrich, born in 1827.

Children:
- Joshua H. Aldrich (1851-1913), bookkeeper, first married Ada E. Lovell (1860-1891), then married Florence (Mahonay?) and moved to Indianapolis, Indiana
- Frank Aldrich (1854-)
- Maria Louise Aldrich (1855-1884)
- Louisa Aldrich (1856-)
- Grace Rogers Aldrich (1861-1930)
- Edward Aldrich (1862-1863)
- Ada Bells Aldrich (1864-1864)

Aldrich had several jobs and positions in the area. In 1861, he was an agent with the Planing Mill Company. By 1865, he had become a captain of a tugboat. In 1867, he is listed as a lumber yard overseer.

Aldrich was a passenger on board the *City of New London* when it sank on November 22, 1871. Mary Jane (Rogers) Aldrich died April 9, 1916.

Matthew W. Baker (1839-1871)   Sect. 88-4

Matthew Wisen Baker, also known as Matthias, was an engineer on board the steamer *City of New London* when it went down in the Thames River on November 22, 1871. He left behind a 5 year old son.

Matthew W. Baker was born September 6, 1839 in Bozrah, Connecticut. His wife, Marynette T. (Rogers) Baker, was born in Connecticut on March 14, 1837, the daughter of Henry Clark Rogers (1804-1865) and Maria Fowler Palmer (1811-1876). Matthew and Marynette were married January 3, 1865 and had one son Matthias Baker, Jr. born December 6, 1865.

Matthew W. Baker died November 22, 1871. His wife, Marynette Baker had died three weeks prior, on October 28, 1871.

William T. Norton (1826-1871)   **Sect. 62-61**

William Tyler Norton died tragically with the burning of the steamship *City of New London,* but some would say he died a hero. It is reported that Norton managed to save the lives of several people before he succumbed in the icy waters.

William Tyler Norton was born December 5, 1826, son of Asa and Sophia (Barker) Norton of Branford, Connecticut. His wife Mary Eliza (Plant) Norton, also of Branford, was born on October 13, 1826. They were married on November 29, 1852.

William Norton, along with his brothers Henry and Timothy, owned and operated the Norton Brothers, a wholesale grocery business in downtown Norwich.

William T. Norton died on November 22, 1871, leaving his wife and three children. Mary Eliza Norton died September 19, 1879.

Caleb B. Rogers (1806-1871)   Sect. 9-6

The Rogers' monument is of marble, with a design unique to this cemetery.

Caleb B. Rogers, or C.B. Rogers as he was also known, was born June 25, 1806, son of Azel Rogers and Sarah (Baker) Rogers. His third wife, Elenora H. Rogers, was born December 23, 1808.

Rogers owned the C.B. Rogers Company, which was listed as "machinists and manufacturers."[1] Two children are listed on the memorial as well: Harriet S. died at two, and Iduella T. who lived to the age of 36.

C.B. Rogers was a passenger on board the *City of New London* when it went down in the Thames River on November 22, 1871.

Caleb B. Rogers was laid to rest November 29, 1871. Elenora H. Rogers died May 10, 1875.

---

1 *Norwich Stedman Directory*, 1866.

XIV.

The Women

Sarah Bowen (ca. 1797-1822)   Sect. 94-1

Although the Yantic Cemetery did not officially open until 1844, this stone dates much earlier than that. The stone reads "Sacred to the Memory of Mrs. SARAH BOWEN, consort of Mr. Augustus Bowen. She died on October 27, 1822, aged 25 years, 4 months, and 12 days."

There does not seem to be much information on Sarah Bowen, but Augustus Bowen is listed in the Norwich census and in the Norwich directories as "accountant" and "bookkeeper." That particular Augustus Bowen was born May 1796 in Rhode Island. He died February 24, 1872.

Mary Collins (1862-1885)   Sect. 115-11

Mary Collins' large and impressive monument was built of granite by Charles Kuebler, a stone cutter who had moved to Norwich from Germany (see the chapter on businessmen).

Not much information is known about Mary Collins, but we do know she was born August 2, 1862. She was the wife of Denis Collins, M.D. Sadly she died in childbirth at the age of 22, along with the child on April 27, 1885.

Mary Congdon (ca. 1811-1864)   Sect. 7-18

Mary Congdon has a most striking monument and it is unique to this cemetery.

Mary (Babcock) Congdon was the wife of William H. Congdon. Mary was born circa 1811. William and Mary were married August 4, 1833 in Norwich by Cornelius B. Everest.

William H. Congdon (1811-1897) was a stonecutter that worked in marble. After the death of his first wife, Mary, he married again, this time to Susan W. Congdon (ca. 1829-1894). His marble stone cutting business was located at various locations in town: on Thames Street, downtown Norwich, at 13 Lafayette Street (near the cemetery), and the business finally relocated to Town Street in Norwichtown.

Mary died April 16, 1864 at the age of 53.

Sarah Larned Osgood (ca. 1819-1891)   Sect. 63

In February 2010, Sarah's memorial was stolen. Somehow the young men managed to wrestle the monument from its base. They cut it into several pieces, including beheading the statue. But the memorial was magnificently repaired and returned to her eternal vigil. This is one of the most impressive and poignant monuments in the Yantic Cemetery.

Sarah (Larned) Osgood was born in Connecticut circa 1819. She married Dr. Charles Osgood, a physician and wholesale druggist in Norwich (his story is listed in the chapter on doctors).

Children:
- Thomas L. Osgood (1840-1841)
- C. Henry Osgood (1842-1925), worked as a clerk in the drugstore
- Frederic L. Osgood (ca. 1849-1923), bookkeeper (probably for his father), chief of police in Norwich (1884-1885), married Eliza White (1848-1924)
- Cornelia Osgood (born ca. 1855), married Col. Augustus C. Tyler (son of Gen. Daniel Tyler), made their home in New London, Connecticut

Dr. Charles Osgood died March 8, 1881 at the age of 73. Sarah followed him in death ten years later on September 11, 1891.

Adelaide W. Peckham, M.D. (1848-1944)   Sect. 43-1

Dr. Adelaide Ward Peckham received her degree as Doctor of Medicine in 1886 from the Women's Medical College of the New York Infirmary.   She also graduated in 1902 from the Women's Medical College of Pennsylvania, the oldest medical college for women in the world.

After graduation, she worked for six years with the University of Pennsylvania, and continued her education in pathology at Johns Hopkins University.   She became a professor of bacteriology at the Women's College in Pennsylvania and director of the clinical lab at the Women's Hospital of Philadelphia.

Dr. Adelaide Ward Peckham was born in Lebanon, Connecticut on March 31, 1848, the daughter of Robert Congdon Peckham (1811-1898) and Sarah Ann Segar (1813-1889).   She attended private schools in Connecticut and New York before making her way into medical schools.

Dr. Peckham died May 13, 1944 in Bloomfield, New Jersey at the age of 96.

Lillian May (Underwood) Spalding (1869-1895)

According to one dictionary, *statuesque* means "possessing great formal beauty or dignity". That certainly describes this monument.

Lillian May (Underwood) Spalding was born May 4, 1869, the daughter of Thomas S. Underwood (1848-1939) and Susan Baron (1832-1926). The census report of 1870 lists Thomas' occupation as "house painter."

Lillian married Will S. Spalding. In the 1895 *Norwich Stedman Directory,* it states that he worked for the "N.S.G. Company." Nathan S. Gilbert was a cabinet maker, and Will Spalding worked for him for a number of years.

Lillian died February 4, 1895 at the age of 26. Will S. Spalding died July 10, 1943.

XV.

White Bronze Monuments

White Bronze Monuments

In many of the older cemeteries, there is a type of grave marker or monument that stands out from the rest. These are the silver bluish-gray 'stones' that aren't really stones at all. They are metal. These memorials have stood the test of time. They have that unmistakable silver-grey-blue patina that is recognized immediately. They come in many shapes and sizes, and there are a number of examples in the Yantic cemetery. Some are small, some are quite large, and some are used merely as cornerstones for the plot as pictured here.

The following photographs show the various metal monuments that are found throughout the Yantic Cemetery.

Carrie C. Coit Spalding – Sect. 66-12

Sylvanus Wight; Civil War Soldier – Sect. 49-15

Gardner family stone – Sect. 129-11

Markers from the Gardner plot – Sect. 129-11

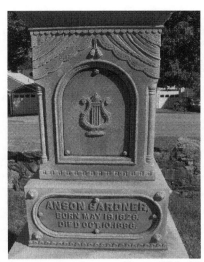

Anson Gardner – Sect. 129-11

John Burdick – Sect. 128-6

Wm. P. Potter – Sect. 124-6
One of the tallest, and most impressive of the
white bronze monuments in Yantic.

In 1868, Mr. M.A. Richardson began to research materials for gravestones. Stone ones that he had observed were susceptible to the ravages of time and weather. He chanced upon a demonstration of cast or molded zinc, and began experimenting with making monuments with this type of metal.

In 1874 in Bridgeport, Connecticut, the Monumental Bronze Company was born and was incorporated in 1879. They began manufacturing a metal monument they touted as 'white bronze,' which in essence was a zinc oxide. When exposed to air, they would take on a distinctive bluish-gray look.

The monuments took on a different look after 1879. From 1877 to 1879, the monuments were a smooth, dark-gray surface. After 1879, they began the process that gives them that distinctive silver bluish-gray tone. "The new production process involved sandblasting the fused cast, causing the surface to resemble stone rather than metal and lightening the color."[1]

The salesmen or agents were the ones who sold the monuments. An ad for such agents appeared in the city directories and in the catalog produced by the company. Interestingly enough, rarely do you find a cemetery with more than a few of these monuments. If you do, it is evidence of a *really* good marketing agent.

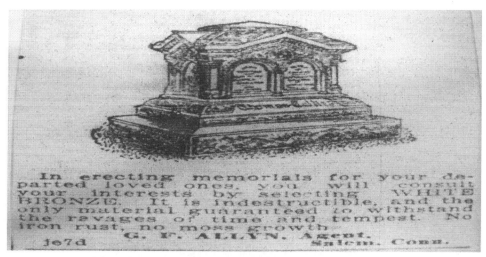

Ad from the *Norwich Bulletin,* Norwich Connecticut, dated 1907.

It is the zinc carbonate that gives the monuments their color. Most markers are either two-sided or four-sided. Each has panels that were made separately and held in place by zinc screws with ornamental heads. Some of the images that one could choose from were: angels, laurels of flowers, sheaves of wheat, bouquet of roses, harps for the music lovers, and many of the monuments were 'draped' at the top with an elaborate drapery motif.

They ranged in size from a few inches to 15 feet tall and ranged in price from $2 to $5,000. There is one that *once stood* 27 feet tall in Schoharie, New York. It

---

1 http://www.civilwarmonument.org/monumental_bronze.htm

included a life-sized statue of the soldier it portrayed. The monument is still there, but without the soldier's likeness.

There were several subsidiaries that were established in the mid-west, including ones in Chicago, Detroit (lasted about four years), Des Moines, Iowa, New Orleans, and St. Thomas, Canada. These 'white bronze' monuments can be found in about 36 states, as well as in Canada, and about 31 of our states boast a Civil War monument made of the same material.

The company only lasted about 40 years, from 1874 to 1914, and ended when the zinc was needed for the war effort. Ironically, the cemetery that boasts the largest number of white bronze statues and monuments is out west; the Riverside Cemetery is located in, of all places, Denver, Colorado.

Once you have seen these markers, you will notice the distinctive color and will probably readily recognize them. So the next time you pass a cemetery, see if you can pick out those distinctive-looking bluish-gray 'stones' that aren't really stones at all.

XVI.

Miscellaneous

William W. Backus (1803-1892)   Sect. 119-13

William Wolcott Backus was born October 22, 1803, the son of James Backus and Dorothy Church Chandler, of Woodstock, Connecticut.

Except for one year in Marietta, Ohio, Backus spent his entire life in Norwich. He had traveled out to Marietta with his kinsman Dudley Woodbridge to set up a mercantile business. He became ill and soon returned home to Norwich.

William Backus was a farmer who raised crops such as Indian corn, rye, potatoes, turnips, and "owned a greater number of horned cattle than any one owner in New London county."[1]

William W. Backus, *History of New London County,* p. 369.

---

1 *History of Norwich, Connecticut*, Francis Caulkins, published 1866, p. 369.

Backus published an exhaustive genealogical family record. He was also a great benefactor. In the late 1800's, with the population growing, two people in particular saw the need for a hospital: William W. Backus and William Albert Slater. Backus donated $75,000 for the purpose of building a hospital, and the hospital bears his name.

William W. Backus died July 13, 1892.

Early postcard of the Backus Hospital, Norwich, Connecticut.

John D. Crocker (1822-1907)   Sect. 36-24

John Denison Crocker was a portrait and landscape artist, as well as an inventor. Many of his paintings can be found in the Slater Museum at the Norwich Free Academy, Norwich, Connecticut.

Born in Salem, Connecticut on November 7, 1822, John was the son of George Crocker (1789-1869) and Nancy Lamphere Crocker (1787-1862). He was one of seven children.

The family moved to Norwich when John was young. His first job was with a wagon maker. He was then apprenticed to a silversmith, but it was while he was working in a furniture shop that he was introduced to the world of portrait painting. Someone had brought in a portrait to be varnished. He was quite taken with the painting and determined to become a portrait painter. He sought out artist Charles Lanman for advice. Although he did a number of portraits, he eventually became most well-known as a landscape artist.

Harriet Elizabeth (Dillaby) Crocker, wife of John Crocker, was born in Connecticut on August 19, 1826, the daughter of Charles Dillaby and Harriet Derby.

Children:

- Harriet Elizabeth Crocker (1850-1909), married Alvan Bussey, overseer of a silk mill, Putnam, Connecticut
- Emma Denison Crocker (1852-1938), married Herman Rallion of Norwich
- John Mozart Crocker (1854-), moved to Derby, Connecticut
- Thomas Cole Crocker (1856-1885), died in Buenos Aires, Argentina in July 1885
- Lillian Huntington Crocker (1858-), married Frank T. Knight, a machinist who worked with the government in Washington, D.C.; in 1910 Frank worked in the Navy Yard; daughter Gladys was a bookbinder with the government printing office
- Rose Blanchard Crocker (1861-1889), married Fred Sharpe who worked for the "M Mfg. Co."* and lived in Putnam
- Charles Dillaby Crocker (1864-1945), married Calista Corbin (1819-1892) and moved to Hartford
- Edward Hosmer Crocker (1867-1956), married Bertha E. Williams (1873-1953) and died in Putnam, Connecticut

John Denison Crocker died September 2, 1907. Harriet E. Crocker died April 29, 1919.

* There was a Monohansett Manufacturing Co. in Putnam, established in 1872, that made cotton goods.

196

John P. Miller (1843-1891)
Herbert T. Miller (1853-1920)   Sect. 103-19

This is a marvelous statue. This beautiful statue holds a scroll, and upon closer examination, one can see that the scroll has a song written on it in musical notation. Although difficult to see here, the song is that of *Auld Lang Syne.*

John P. Miller is one of those listed on this monument. John Porter Miller was born in Franklin, Connecticut on September 12, 1843, the son of Samuel Miller (1815-1872) and Lucy A. Miller (1814-1895). Samuel's occupation is listed as candle wick manufacturer. John's brother, Herbert T. Miller, was born in September 1853. The brothers were both musicians.

John P. Miller, musician and dance master, lived on Oak Street in the Greenville section of Norwich. His wife, Donna M. (Whipple) Miller, was born December 1851 in Connecticut.

John P. Miller died in 1891. In 1894, Donna Miller married John's brother Herbert. Herbert Miller died January 20, 1920. Donna Miller died June 23, 1938.

Joseph Otis (1768-1854) **Sect. 9**

Joseph Otis was born in the Yantic section of Norwich on July 27, 1768, the son of Joseph Otis (1739-1823) and Lucy Houghton (1741-) or Horton as it is sometimes listed. His wife Ann (also known as Nancy) (Huntington) Otis was born May 17, 1772. In 1797, Joseph and Ann were married.

Joseph Otis established the Otis Library in 1848 with the encouragement of his pastor, the Reverend Alvan Bond (found in an earlier section of the book). The architect of the library was Joshua W. Shepard, the local architect/builder who was responsible for the building of at least eight of the thirty plus houses in the Little Plain section of Norwich. The first librarian was H. B. Buckingham. The Otis Library had a room set aside as the Pastor's Study for the pastors of the Second Congregational Church, which was just up the street located on Church Street.

From Alvan Bond's eulogy of Otis, we find that Otis lived in New York a good majority of his life, and that "His position, enterprise, and success, secured for him the respect and confidence of the highest class of merchants..." He returned to Norwich in 1838. Reverend Bond went on to say, "He decided to establish a public library... to enable all classes... to avail themselves of its privileges." "He lived to witness the successful operation of this institution..."[2]

Otis was twelve years old when he began working for a Mr. McCurdy in Norwich, and worked with him for about ten years. He moved to Charleston, South

---

2 *A Discourse on the Life and Character of Dea. Joseph Otis, delivered in the Second Congregational Church, Norwich, Conn., March 19, 1854,* by Alvan Bond, D.D., printed by Andrew Stark, printer, 1855.

Carolina sometime around 1790, and moved to New York in 1796, where he established himself in mercantile pursuits.

Otis and his wife lived in Stratford, Connecticut from 1812 to 1815. During this time and until 1833, he was in business with Asa Otis. With failing health, he returned to Norwich in 1838.

Nancy (Ann) Huntington Otis died August 27, 1844. Joseph Otis died March 11, 1854.

Katie C. Rallion (1878-1889)   Sect. 122-1

It was the portrait of young Katie Corbin Rallion that caught my eye. Her grandfather, John Crocker, whose story is also in this section, painted this portrait of her. Katie, born in 1878, was just 11 years old when she died. She was the daughter of Emma (Crocker) Rallion and Herman D. Rallion, and the granddaughter of the artist John Denison Crocker.

Portrait of Katie Rallion painted by her grandfather, John D. Crocker.

John Denison Crocker was a portrait painter from Norwich, Connecticut. Many of his paintings hang in the Slater Museum at the Norwich Free Academy.

Katie had a sister, Myra, three years older (1875-1961). Their father, Herman D. Rallion, was born October 1847 in Charlton, Massachusetts and their mother, Emma D. Crocker was born in February 1852 in Connecticut. Herman Rallion was in the grocery business most of his working life. In the 1900 census, Myra was working as a bookkeeper, apparently in the business with her father.

For about three years, Herman Rallion was co-owner of the Rallion & Company (Rallion and Kelley) meat market, which was located on Franklin Street, downtown Norwich.

Katie Rallion died on July 27, 1889, and is buried with her family.

Edmund B. Richardson (1822-1901) Section 62-20

The obituary listed in the *Norwich Bulletin* tells the poignant tale of 'E.B.' Richardson and his wife Harriet. Harriet Richardson had died on March 10, 1901 in California while on a trip and was buried there. Edmund had traveled to Riverside, California in December of that year to retrieve her body and bring her back to Norwich to be re-interred in the Yantic Cemetery. But before he could do that, he himself was killed in a trolley accident on Christmas Day 1901 in Riverside, California. Both bodies were then brought back together and a joint funeral was held. The January 1902 Norwich Bulletin obituary states that "a committal service [was] being read by the Reverend J. Eldred Brown of Trinity Episcopal church."

Edmund B. Richardson was born in 1822 in Connecticut. His wife, Harriet (Jewett) Richardson, was born in Connecticut in 1828. Both of their children, Edmund B. Richardson Jr (born June 12, 1848) and Harriet E. Richardson (born circa April 1850), were born in Massachusetts.

At the time of his son's birth in 1848, Richardson was listed as an auctioneer, but in the 1861 *Norwich Stedman Directory*, he is listed as owning his own company, Richardson & Company, "manufacturer of Dr. Sweet's Liniment," located on Water Street, downtown Norwich.

Edmund and Harriet Richardson were interred together in the Yantic Cemetery on January 4, 1902.

Edmund B. Richardson, Jr.
(aka Edmund Bradley) (1838-1877) **Sect. 62-20**

Edmund Bradley Richardson, Jr., who called himself Edmund Bradley, died on September 25, 1877 in the battle of Cow Creek in the area of Fort Benton, Montana.

"Bradley, Edmund, a young black American, was a skilled carpenter and house builder. In 1877 he lived in Fort Benton with his Gros Ventre Native American wife and young daughter. Bradley was killed in the Cow Creek Canyon fight on September 25. [Aka E. B. Richardson]"[3]

Edmund Bradley had been recruited by the commander of the military post at Fort Benton, Montana, Major Guido Ilges. He joined forces with about 50 civilian volunteers to assist the small detachment of the 7th Infantry Regiment "assigned to protect a large cache of steamboat freight at Cow Island on the Missouri River."[4]

Bradley was killed in a skirmish. Major Ilges ordered that his body be returned to Fort Benton. The local newspaper "The River Press" covered the impressive funeral:

3 Blackamericansmt.blogspot.com/2009/12/on-being-black-american-in-territorial_29.html
4 Ibid.

203

The funeral of the lamented volunteer, killed in the Cow Creek fight on the 24th of September last, took place on Saturday, the 8th inst. The remains were followed to the grave by nearly all the residents of the town, including the Home Guards, commanded by Captain John Evans, the volunteers who participated in the gallant fight at Cow Creek, and the soldiers from the military post. A number of ladies were also present at the grave. The coffin was covered with black velvet and tastefully trimmed with black fringe and silver mountings. The procession, commanded by Major Guido Ilges, 7th Infantry, fell into line at fifteen minutes past 1 o'clock, p.m. There was no confusion, loud talking or other disturbance, but all present seemed deeply impressed with the solemnity of the occasion. When the command, 'Forward, march,' was given, the line moved off in the following order, to the sound of a muffled drum: Fife and drum. Firing party, consisting of eight soldiers from the military post. Hearse bearing coffin covered with United States flag. Party of fifty citizens, on foot. Volunteers and home Guards, mounted, about forty in number. Six wagons, containing county officials and other invited guests. On arriving at the cemetery, the coffin was first placed beside and afterward[s] lowered into the grave. The funeral service was read in a very impressive manner by Mr. J. A. Kanouse, while all present stood with uncovered heads. After the service the firing party discharged three volleys over the grave, which completed the funeral ceremony and the honors to the dead.[5]

Edmund Bradley Richardson was the son of Edmund B. Richardson and Harriet (Jewett) Richardson. His wife was of the Gros Ventre tribe of Native Americans, whom he married while at Fort Benton. They reportedly had two children, a son Steve, and a daughter Ann. The son and the mother stayed on the reservation with the mother's family after Bradley was killed. There was a report that Edmund's mother had met up with the little girl in Bismarck, North Dakota. Ann apparently came back to Norwich to reside with the grandmother, for she is found with the Richardson family in the 1880 census of Norwich.

A year after the burial at the fort, the body of Edmund Bradley was exhumed and shipped back to Connecticut via the steamboat *Colonel Macleod* and turned over to his mother in New Haven. His journey continued on to Norwich, probably by train, and burial took place in September 1878.

In the Indian census roll of 1930, Steven Bradley was living at Fort Belnap Indian Reservation, Montana and was listed as head of house with a wife, Margaret (Shining Face), a Gros Ventre tribal member. Two children are listed to them. William was born circa 1913 and Rufus was born circa 1920.

Edmund Bradley (Richardson), Jr. was laid to rest in the Yantic Cemetery on September 21, 1878.

---

5 From the website: http://fortbenton.blogspot.com/2006_07_25_archive.html

Stephen B. Roath (1829-1905)   Sect. 34-10

Stephen Billings Roath left quite a legacy with family and friends. It was always thought by his family that he was rather poor, since he maintained the simplest of lifestyles. But at the end of his life he came back to Norwich after living in Chicago for most of his adult life and doled out to his family $1,000,000 while he was still living.

Stephen Roath was born in Norwich on March 7, 1829, the son of Asa Roath and Elizabeth (Allyn) Roath. He began as an engine driver for the Norwich and Worcester Railroad. In 1854, at the age of 23, he moved out to Chicago. By 1870, he was working for the Union Stockyards as a clerk and bookkeeper. By 1889, his occupation is listed as capitalist.

Roath moved back to Norwich in July of 1904, and lived out the rest of his life in his hometown. He hired Stephen Meech, the president of the Thames Bank, to see to his financial affairs and assist in doling out the money. He was quoted as saying, "I have had fun accumulating the money... now I want to see what my relatives will do with it."[6]

Stephen Roath died February 14, 1905.

---

6 From an article attached to his FindAGrave.com page entitled *"Wants to Die Poor,"* dated September 3, 1903, paper Aberdeen Daily News, Aberdeen, South Dakota.

At this writing, there is no stone for David Ruggles, but evidence indicates he is buried with his family in the Ruggles family plot.

David Ruggles was an abolitionist, journalist, editor and a major conductor in the Underground Railroad. David Ruggles was a black man born in Norwich, Connecticut on March 15, 1810, the son of David and Nancy Ruggles. His father was a blacksmith and his mother was well-known for her cakes and homemade goods.

The family settled in the Bean Hill section of Norwich. Church was a large part of their family life. Schooling was also an important part of his life in Norwich. One of his teachers was the author and poetess Lydia Huntley Sigourney. As the author Graham Russell Gao Hodges states, "... he came out of the Norwich schools highly literate and versed in classical and sacred literature."[7]

Children of David and Nancy Ruggles:
- **David Ruggles (1810-1849)**
- Livinia Ruggles, b. 1814
- Felix Ruggles (1817-1862)
- Thomas Ruggles, b. 1819
- George Ruggles, b. 1821
- Henry Ruggles, b. 1825
- Richard Ruggles, b. 1827
- Frances Jane Ruggles, b. 1832

David moved to New York City at the age of 17, first working as a seaman, eventually opening a grocery store. He started out selling liquor, but after a time, he joined the temperance movement and removed hard drink from his inventory.

In 1834, David Ruggles opened the first black bookstore in New York City; one year later it was burned by a mob of whites. He relocated and continued his campaign against slavery.

He assisted many, many people on their road to freedom. One such person was Frederick Douglass, the African-American leader of the abolitionist movement.

David Ruggles died December 16, 1849.

---

7 *David Ruggles A Radical Black Abolitionist and the Underground Railroad in New York City,* Graham Russell Gao Hodges, University of North Carolina Press, Chapel Hill, p. 18.

George F. Ulmer (1874-1907)   Sect. 30-5

George Frederick Ulmer died by his own hand at the age of 33 in Crockett, California on August 29, 1907. He was a chemist, and had been living in Brooklyn, New York and working at the Arbuckle Refinery. He moved to the San Francisco area and began working for the C&H Sugar Refinery in Crockett, touted as the largest refinery in the world.

George Ulmer, the son of Frank Ulmer (1845-1903) and Eleanore (Frickmann) Ulmer (1850-1905), was born in Preston, Connecticut on June 14, 1874. Both his parents were born in Germany.

In 1894, his father, Frank Ulmer, was the president of the W.H. Davenport Fire Arms Company. A short time later, the family (father Frank and brother Henry F.) owned the Ulmer Leather Company, which were manufacturers of leather belting.

Children of Frank and Eleanore Ulmer:
- Henry Ulmer (b. ca. 1869), assisted his father in the Ulmer Leather Co.
- **George Ulmer (1874-1907)**
- Johanna C. Ulmer (b. ca. 1877)
- Eleonore F. Ulmer (b. ca. 1881)

By 1900, George had moved to New York to work in the Arbuckle Sugar Refinery located at 10 Jay Street, Brooklyn. By 1903, he had made his way out to California. In January 1907, he became the superintendent of the C&H sugar refinery in Crockett, California.

The evening before his death, he had conferred with two of his friends in the Hotel Crockett, where he had expressed despondency and uncertainties about his position at the refinery. Although the friends assured him that he was doing a fine job and he was well-liked at the company, he shot himself in his hotel room in the early morning hours of August 29, 1907.

It was said by his friends that he had a head injury a number of years before when he was thrown from a horse. Again just prior to his death, he had a similar accident which supposedly "aggravated the old brain trouble and led to the suicide."[8]

George F. Ulmer was laid to rest September 9, 1907.

---

8 *San Francisco Chronicle,* dated August 30, 1907.

Theophilus Y. Winship (1820-1913)   Sect. 18-2

Theophilus Yale Winship was born in September 1820 in Connecticut, son of Captain Thomas D. Winship of New York and Phila Yale of Connecticut. Theophilus' wife, Jerusha Adelaide Avery, born in August 1824, was also from Connecticut. They were married in 1850. In the 1860's, they made their home in the East Great Plains area of Norwich.

There is a grandfather's clock in the Faith Trumbull Chapter of the Daughters of the American Revolution Museum in this city that Mr. Winship had given to his wife. She was ill at the time and thought it looked too much like a coffin so she had it put into an outbuilding where she would not have to look at it. It sat there for many years, and eventually found its way to the museum.

In the 1860's, Winship is listed as a grocer, but by 1870 he had become a farmer and continued that until his death in 1913.

In 1900, Theophilus and Jerusha celebrated 50 years of marriage.

Jerusha Winship died June 2, 1906. Theophilus Yale Winship died March 18, 1913.

ACKNOWLEDGEMENTS

I would like to thank the following people for their help and encouragement during the researching and writing of this book. First my husband, Bob, for his long-suffering patience during the whole process. Next, I would like to thank the Otis Library Staff for all their assistance during the research and also the Norwich Historical Society for their encouragement. More encouragement came from all the friends and family who listened to 'one more story.' And finally, I would like to thank my editor, Lynn Whiteford, for all her hard work making this book flow so well and my publisher Glenn Cheney at New London Librarium for helping to make this happen.

ABOUT THE AUTHOR

Melodye A. Whatley was born in California, but raised mostly in Oklahoma and Texas. Like so many, she came to Connecticut because of the Navy and settled in Norwich. Melodye and her husband both came to Connecticut with a love of history. In the mid-80's, she and her family became involved with historical reenactments portraying the Revolutionary War era. Melodye and her husband were caretakers of the Daughters of the American Revolution Museum in Norwich for several years. During that time, Melodye became interested in the Yantic Cemetery, having taken some of the cemetery walks led by David Oat. Exploring the cemetery on her own, she began reading tombstones, and just *had* to know the stories.

Made in the USA
Middletown, DE
14 April 2019